TABLE OF

Hedley Brass Band, 1914

Acknowledgements

We owe a huge debt of gratitude to the late Philip J. Thomas, for without him this book would never have been written. Phil Thomas collected songs in BC between 1949 and 1985. He was the first song collector in Canada to place the songs firmly in their social-historical contexts and he took great pains in his search for accuracy. His book *Songs of the Pacific Northwest* is a seminal work. We knew Phil Thomas and worked with him since the 1960s and have over the years learned and sung the songs he collected many times. We hope that in the process we have absorbed his unerring instinct for what constitutes a "true" song. As we work we feel him looking over our shoulders. We also feel that we are standing on his shoulders and continuing his work in collecting and disseminating BC's vernacular cultural history.

We found the rich store of songs and poems that appear here lodged in the comprehensive newspaper collection of the Princeton Archives. Our first introduction to the Archives was through Nick Mills, at that time the Manager. We thank him for introducing us to this fabulous resource and we thank the Princeton and District Museum and Archives Society for the continued maintenance of the newspaper collection, now housed in the newly refurbished Museum.

Two people made this manuscript into a book. Allison Campbell read the whole manuscript and helped us immensely with historical and editorial suggestions: if the prose flows smoothly and the explanations make sense, it is thanks largely to her input. Ginger Erskine, our book designer, used her artistic skills to transform the manuscript into an elegant book. Our great thanks to them both.

We thank Theresa Thomas and the late Mildred Bains, daughters of Phil Thomas, who gave us generous access to Phil's books, papers and photographs. We are grateful to Brenda Gould, archaeologist for the Upper Similkameen Indian Band, for her historical advice. Coalmont historians Bob and Diane Sterne were most generous with information about Coalmont and Granite Creek, as was Princeton's Terry Malanchuk in sharing his expertise about Blakeburn. Lori Thomas and Dawn Johnson, descendants of Princeton pioneers, were always very gracious about answering historical questions whenever we asked them.

We thank Hedley Museum for generous access to their archives and the use of many fine photographs, and we thank our friend Stuart James for his critical ear and unerring support as we worked to bring this project to fruition.

Horses and wagons at Hedley Stamp Mill

Preface

Social history is the hardest history to write. The resources a social historian can draw on are often opaque, often fragmentary. Diaries and memoirs are the chief sources, together with broad-based statistics (of health and education and the like). Oftentimes novels can provide a glimpse into the era in which they were written. But to bring this material together and to make of such disparate parts a narrative that properly reflects the experience of people requires an awareness of a broad range of cultural issues and concerns – famous sporting events, the impact of national and regional politics, the accidents of public life such as fire and flood, and the unpredictable events of family life.

In this book we have chosen to visit the Similkameen valley, in the southern interior of British Columbia, between the years 1900 and 1950, and have used as our source for this visit the newspapers published there. We have read every copy of every paper, and have focused our attention on the most ephemeral material found there – the verses and songs that were to be found in most local newspapers in BC (and probably the whole of western North America) in such profusion in those years. It is through this material that we hope to gain an understanding of the lived experience of the valley's population.

Why did we choose this ephemera, when so much other newspaper material was to hand? We chose it because it was ephemeral, or, in another sense, trivial. The ideas expressed in the verses, like the newspapers themselves, are only for the moment. There is little attempt on the part of the versifiers to strike heroic poses – in fact, the opposite is more nearly true. The language is often both sly and ironic. But because it is only here for the moment, it must be fresh. And it must reflect (as more authored material, such as books, made "for the ages", does not) the passions of the moment. It can thus help us to gain an imaginative appreciation of the lived experience.

The poems we selected were those that addressed issues of concern to people in the valley. We tried as much as possible to choose verses that were made locally and that spoke about topics specific to the area. We did not include generic love poetry or overblown Victorian nature poetry and we left out a number of patriotic verses. In order to provide an historical and social context for the verses, we have organized them thematically into chapters.

The period from 1850 to 1914 -- the Victorian and Edwardian eras -- was a time of huge social and technological change. It included Canadian Confederation in 1867 and BC's entry into Confederation in 1871, and saw the emergence of railways, electricity, telephones, radios, automobiles, phonographs, movies and air travel. It also included the settlement of western North America and the creation of towns. It was a time of optimism and immense economic growth, spurred by the discovery of new resources, massive immigration and improved transportation. The First World War brought a sudden end to this period of growth and in western Canada such prosperity did not return until the 1950s. The collection of poems and songs presented in this book covers this tumultuous period. Even though the collection does not begin until 1900, the date of the first newspaper in the valley, the sensibility of people in the area remained Victorian and Edwardian long after the reigns of those monarchs. The predominantly British population living here in colonial isolation created a cultural world that would not have been unfamiliar to a 19th century Brit. Even when immigrants of other nationalities began arriving in large numbers to work in the mines -- Italians, Slovaks and the like -- public culture remained predominantly British. The limitation of this collection is therefore that it lacks the voices of these minorities. In spite of this limitation we hope that the voices of the verses in this collection provide a "snapshot" of life in the Upper Similkameen during the first half of the 20th century.

We came to this task through our work as singers and teachers, particularly of the songs of BC. We know these songs thanks to the work of the late Philip J. Thomas, who travelled the province between the years 1954 and 1975 collecting what were commonly called "folk songs". These songs were made mostly by loggers, miners and fisherfolk, and they provide their own popular people's history of BC, through the development of those industries. The people Phil Thomas collected from created and shared their songs at a time before radio and recorded music had suffused our aural environment, a time when ordinary people sang together and made up their own songs. These people are no longer with us and those that followed don't carry a trove of aural culture in their heads anymore. In fact, Thomas's collecting work could not be done today. His book, *Songs of the Pacific Northwest,* is a monument to BC's sung heritage.

Thomas made several song-collecting trips to the Similkameen valley in the 1960s. The songs he collected from the singing of such people as Bob Baird, Art Shenton and Bill Frew are a snapshot of the daily life of people in the valley and are part of the area's cultural and occupational heritage.

Thomas collected some twenty songs in the area. On the premise that there might be more, we began the search in 2006 through the local newspapers housed in the Princeton Archives, where we found not only songs but also a great number of verses. They spoke of the everyday concerns of the people of the Similkameen - enduring the loneliness of immigration, the long winters, paying off debts, working in a mine, waiting for the railway to come, losing a son in the war or fixing an old car. These were the voices of the valley. Furthermore, they spoke in the style we were familiar with through Thomas' collecting. Compare, for example,

> Some say it's luck, but that's all bunk –
> Why, he was doing business when the times were punk.
> People have to purchase and the geezer was wise –
> For he knew the way to get 'em was to advertise.

from a 1916 copy of the *Similkameen Star*, with

They stand by the cold deck, a-wasting my time
Not setting no chokers, nor tending no line
When up comes a fella and he says, "I suppose
You work on the riggin' by the looks of your clothes."

from the Thomas collection.

The Thomas piece is a re-working of Curly Fletcher's "The Strawberry Roan", a well-known western song, of which Fletcher himself says, "Most of [my] work is in the vernacular of these early pioneers of the traditional West. The phrases and idioms are a part of everyday conversations, which are still common among these virile, independent, free-hearted, generous men and women …", words which could well describe not merely the first piece but much of what we have included here.

Our urban-based consumer society has by and large lost any connection with the land; we are creatures of text and the internet, always "somewhere else", which is where most of our songs come from, too. In contradistinction, many of the songs and verses in this collection reflect an intimate connection to the landscapes and physical character of the Similkameen valley. The particularity of named towns, creeks, rivers and mountains allows us to remake this intimate connection. We can recapture that intimacy with the landscape, which the early settlers in the Similkameen surely shared, through the immediacy of their verse and song, such as that in Thomas's book and this collection of verses.

....

A number of years ago some friends told us of driving home to the coast over the Hope-Princeton Highway. They were playing our CD, "Now It' s Called Princeton: Songs and Poems of BC's Upper Similkameen". At the site of the Hope Slide, some 19 kilometers east of Hope, they stopped and played Paddy Graber's song, which recounts what happened when the mountain collapsed in January 1965. Our friends told us that their children were amazed that there was a song about the place, and that they suddenly looked at the landscape with new eyes. Our hope is that the readers of this book will similarly see the Similkameen valley with new eyes.

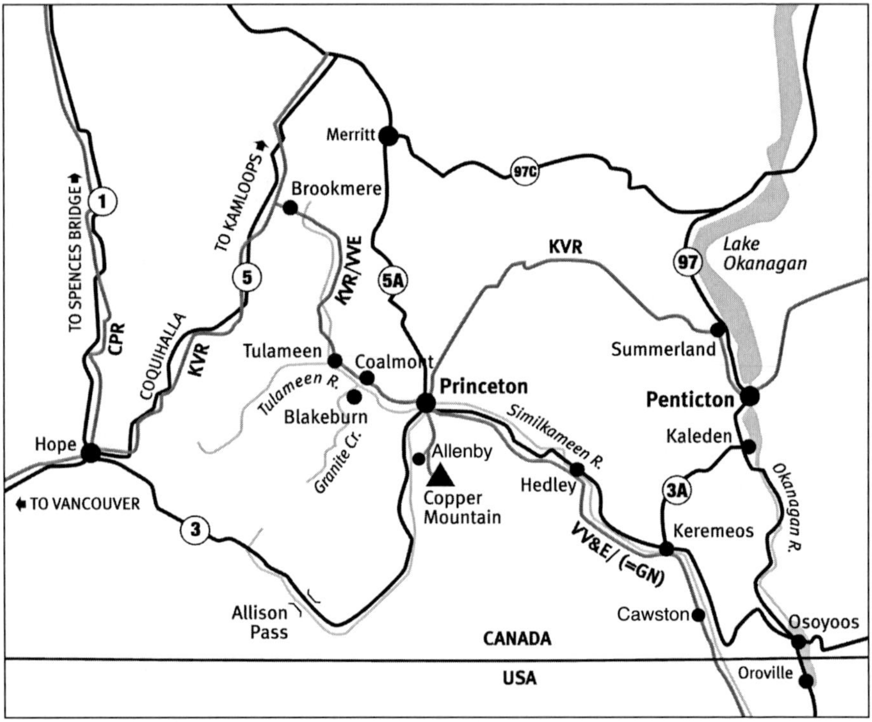

KVR	Kettle Valley Railway
VV & E	Vancouver, Victoria & Eastern Railway
GN	Great Northern Railway
CPR	Canadian Pacific Railway

Chapter 1: Popular Song and Verse Traditions of the Early 20th Century

We speak of "verse" here rather than "poetry", because the word "poem" suggests a more formal and emotional content that that typically found in newspapers. "Verse" suggests, firstly, a rhyme, and secondly, a meter; and the verses printed here have both.

Verse was very commonly found in 19th and early 20th century schools. Schoolchildren of that era were taught to memorize verse and poetry, and it had a much larger place in the world than it does today. Many people of that era had thousands of lines in their head, which they could (and often would) recite at informal concerts, school recitals and "smokers" (informal social gatherings for men). Field Marshal Lord Wavell, the British Army commander, edited an anthology in 1944 titled *Other Men's Flowers*, comprising some 260 poems and verses he had memorized, which he himself thought was not an unusual number. The book is still in print, evidence that his selection reflected in the main the preferences and choices of his contemporaries (and of their children, who were familiar with their parents' recitations).

Verse is easier to remember than prose, and song (verses with music) even easier. Many of those who memorized poems and verses at school can still remember them seventy and eighty years later. Verses, too, oftentimes can carry a freight of meaning that would be hard for prose to carry, and at the same time can be as lightweight as:

> God in his wisdom made the fly
> And then forgot to tell us why.

Several of the verses in this collection are actually songs, and there are many more that might have had a tune to them. Often the structure of the verse will suggest the tune, as in

> How dear to my heart my remembrance of milling

(the first line of The Hangup Stick)

A clear parody of

> How dear to my heart are the scenes of my childhood

… the opening line of "The Old Oaken Bucket", a tear-jerker of 1817, and still widely-known a century later.

A Shared Culture

People who have grown up in the same culture can share that culture for a lifetime, without ever stepping out of it. What do you say when someone sneezes? What do you sing on someone's birthday? What does walking under a ladder signify? The answer to these questions is automatic if you belong to the predominant culture. Poems and songs "which everyone knows" are the bedrock of this type of culture, found now in Canada only in Quebec and in some parts of the Atlantic provinces. (Try, for example, to think of a song that "everybody" in BC knows). Of course, even in those places, not "everyone" knows these pieces, but to recite or to sing them is to proclaim that you belong to the culture. This is the informal pattern: the formal pattern is the National Anthem, and additionally in the United States, the recitation of the Pledge of Allegiance. These are formal markers of a shared culture and are typical examples of those elements of the culture which some people think everyone *should* know. We call this "received" culture.

You acquire your culture from a variety of sources. Firstly, of course, is the family. What your parents thought, talked about, recited or sang became part of your own culture. The family folklore (about Uncle Albert, or about what names you give to your cats, dogs or horses) is also included here. Next is school – a formal culture, through school books, of received poetry, verse, songs, novels, and history, and an informal culture of play; the counting-out rhymes ("One potato, two potato"), the kid-made parodies of the received culture ("While Shepherds Washed Their Socks by Night"), and the rules of the school games. Church, too, is a common source. In those days, the Church Year (Advent, Christmas, Lent, Easter, Whitsun), which generated the legal year and the school year, governed much more of the daily round, and Sunday School was much more commonly attended. Its hymns, too, provided weekly practice in community singing, its bells created an aural pattern for the day, and its ceremonies (baptism, confirmation, marriage, and death) punctuated most people's lives.

There is also a political culture. Canadians thought (and still think) of themselves as living in a democracy, where they could think and say what they thought (within the limits of the obscenity and blasphemy laws). They did not have to keep their voices down when passing a policeman, and they felt free to comment, in prose or in verse, on whatever they liked. People were in theory equal -- with the important exceptions of First Nations people, Chinese people, women and those under 21, none of whom could vote.

These cultural sources (parents, church, school) are, in a manner of speaking, timeless. Though they change, they do so very slowly. Were these the only sources, life for us would be similar to the lives experienced by our parents and grandparents. But there is another source with infinitely greater power to change the culture, and that is the culture of the outside world. This culture (though it is of course composed of many different subcultures) is what makes for vast and fast changes. A popular music industry developed over the course of the 19th century. It was most powerful in cities, where people could attend concerts, music halls, and vaudeville. In rural communities, where these were often absent, the only source was sheet music, and word of mouth from someone who had been to the city. It was the phonograph and the radio which finally put an end to what a German philosopher called "the idiocy of rural life". The first phonograph advertisement in the Princeton paper was in 1919, the first feature length movie ad in 1921 (D.W. Griffith's "The Love Flower") and the first radio advertisement in 1924. In the years that followed, people were less likely to make their own songs and music, and more likely to sing or play (or more commonly, merely listen to) a recorded singer or musician. TV had a similar effect, transforming the nation from sports-playing people to sports-watching people.

In the Similkameen in the early years of the 20th century, verses and songs were shared at all the social events - Burns' Night suppers, Elks' and Masons' dinners, Christmas concerts and celebrations, New Years' Masquerade Balls, Rebekah's and Bachelor's Balls, May, Victoria, Labour, Dominion and Independence Day celebrations and Chautauquas, at musical reviews, and at school concerts. Often called "party pieces", for which some persons became known, they had their origin in the shared culture or in locally-made parodies of pieces of the shared culture. The Christmas Eve Concert described in the 29 December 1900 edition of the *Similkameen Star*, for example, featured the following selections (with their creation dates, where available): "O Come All ye Faithful" (a well-known hymn, 1852), "Christmas in the Antipodes", "Merry Christmas Bells" (a popular song, 1875), "Working Out the Dead Horse on the Tulameen" (a local song, with its origins in 1891), "Mystic Star", "Write me a Letter from Home" (a popular song by William Hays of the 1860s), "A Soldier's Sweetheart", and "O Beautiful Star".

The poems and songs found in these pages represent the shared culture of a period from 1900 to 1945. After the Second World War this culture began to wane. Media such as radio and TV did their part in helping the decay, with the replacement of local and particular cultures with a national and ultimately international -- mostly American -- culture. School curricula changed, and the introduction of formal multiculturalism in the 1960s argued for the recognition of other strands of Canadian experience, in addition to the British Isles-based culture. But the Similkameen valley was slower than other parts of BC to adapt to the new cultural mix, partly because of its isolation. Radio and TV were late coming to the valley, and people in the early years of the 20th century were left to their own devices much more than we are today.

Social and Cultural Context of the Verses

The verses and songs collected here were all published in Similkameen valley newspapers from 1900 to 1950, but they came from many different places. Some are drawn from the work of published poets, some from vaudeville and the popular stage, some were made anonymously, either in the valley or elsewhere, using a well-known piece of verse or song as a base, and some were composed locally "from scratch". This also describes of the origin of the songs collected by Phil Thomas and published in his *Songs of the Pacific Northwest.* He was looking for what was sung before the songs made popular by radio began seriously to overwhelm the home-grown material. Most people learn the songs they carry through their lives before the age of eighteen, and so, since radio arrived in BC in the late 'twenties, Thomas's informants were born before the turn of the century, and thus when he collected from them, they were between the ages of 60 and 90.

These people are no longer with us, and the stories they shared in song were of an earlier BC, a BC in its formative years. They belonged to a generation which saw the BC population double in nine years, from 130,000 in 1895 to 264,000 in 1905. This was the era of development throughout southern BC and the catalyst was mining. All the communities in the valley, with the exception of Keremeos, were mining towns. To the town came men looking to stake a claim or looking for work. They brought with them their own home cultures, and those cultures were reflected in the local newspapers.

Or were they? The *Similkameen Star* gives the population of Princeton in 1918 as around 1,000, with 530 being described as "white" and the balance as "foreigners" ("Italians 100, Scandinavians 125, Chinese 80, Austrians 25, Doukhobors 120, others 20"). "White" in this context clearly means "of British stock". These foreigners and their lived experiences are almost totally absent from the pages of

Princeton's newspaper, except as figures of fun and fear. We shall get a better understanding of the population and where it came from when the 1921 Census is released in 2013.

Newspapers acted as an amplifier of the received culture; in order of "respectability", that of the British Isles (Scots, English, Welsh, Irish, in that order), then northern European (Swedish, Norwegian, Danish, Dutch, German), then southern European (French, Italian, Spanish), then – a long way back in respectability – Eastern Europeans (Slavs, Croats, Slovenes). Not connected to the town in any recognizably cultural way were the Chinese, alternately joked about or hated or feared, and First nations people, who appeared as "local colour" on special occasions, such as Victoria Day or Dominion Day. The shared culture was entirely a British culture, and those to whom it was unknown were themselves "unknown" by the town. Of course, each cultural group in Princeton shared a culture, but these cultures were invisible to the mainstream British-based culture, which produced (and read) the papers that made up our sources.

Princeton Hockey Team, 1915. Princeton Museum

Chapter 2: The Settlement of the Similkameen

The settlement of the Similkameen, as with all settlement, was determined by landscape, climate and resources. The decline of the fur trade in the middle of the 19th century coincided with the arrival of settlers in the valley, most of whom came to ranch on the rangeland of the interior. They came to an unfamiliar landscape and climate, often with little or no ranching experience. **A Song of BC** makes fun of such a settler, an upper class British greenhorn who begs for help from his uncle, the earl. Such people were sometimes referred to as "remittance men" (who survived financially on a regular remittance from home) or as the "Haw Haw, By Jove variety of Englishman".

The discovery of coal, gold, platinum and copper sparked the second wave of settlement and the establishment of towns. The establishment of the upper Similkameen towns of Hedley, Princeton, Coalmont, Tulameen, Copper Mountain and Allenby followed the pattern so well established in the west Kootenay region. That pattern led in many cases to ghost towns when the ore was played out or when digging for it became uneconomical. Princeton was saved from this fate because of the continued background of ranching and by a ready timber supply, which provided jobs in forestry.

The Early Years

Dark forests and precipitous mountains engulf the traveller going east from Hope. There is little sun or sky to light the way, until, some twenty kilometers west of Princeton, the landscape suddenly opens up. Sunny vistas invite the eye as the Hope Mountains are left behind and one enters the open terrain of the Similkameen valley. John Fall Allison, travelling this route in 1858, must have felt huge relief after struggling through deadfall and devil's club to find himself in these sunny uplands.

The Similkameen River rises in the Hope Mountains -- part of the Cascade Range -- and flows into Princeton fifty kilometers from the American border. The Tulameen River, flowing from the northwest through Tulameen and Coalmont, joins it there. From Princeton, the Similkameen flows southeast through Hedley, Keremeos and Cawston and then crosses into the US, where it joins the Okanagan River, which itself joins the Columbia. The Similkameen valley is at the southwestern edge of BC's semi-arid interior plateau and is characterized by rolling grasslands and sunny weather.

At the time of John Fall Allison's arrival, the Similkameen valley was inhabited by about 200 members of the nomadic Chuchuwayha branch of the Similkameen Nicola Indians. They had encampments up and down the valley and lived by trapping, hunting and fishing. Fur traders had travelled through the valley since the second decade of the century but no one settled here until Allison began ranching and small-scale placer mining in the early 1860s. At that time he lived with his Indian common law wife, Nora Yakumtikum, with whom he had four children. In 1867, Allison brought his bride, Susan, to the Similkameen -- she was the first white woman to cross the Hope Mountains -– and together they raised fourteen children. Neighbours were few and far between and John Fall Allison was often away. Susan Allison's sentiments must often have resembled those of the author of **In My Dreams** who longed for his "dear old English home". But not everyone longed for the "ivy covered" cottages of the Old Country. Arthur Stringer, author of **The Greater Briton In England** felt claustrophobic there and longed for the "outland trail, the upward sweep," and the "widening dawn" of the "New World".

Susan Allison's primary companions during those early years were Indians. In 1915, Estelle Kerr wrote in the *Similkameen Star*:

> Mrs. Allison was the friend of the Indians, and they trusted her and told her stories, which she translated into English verse. Her principal work, "In-cow-masket," is a tale of a chief of that name, and of his wives and children.

"In-cow-masket" is strongly modelled on Longfellow's "Hiawatha". **The Naming of the Similkameen** by Fred Stamper lightly satirizes this romantic version of the "noble savage".

Despite loneliness and hardships, Susan Allison stayed in the Similkameen. Her ambivalent relationship to the landscape in which she lived is expressed in her poem **Evening on the Similkameen** (published under her nom de plume "Stratton Moir", the name of her late father as well as her late brother). Estelle Kerr expressed her admiration for Susan Allison:

> A poetess in Princeton! Walk along the main street and pity her, climb the hills and envy her, for if ever a little western mining town had an ideally beautiful situation, it is Princeton.

These sentiments are echoed by Dave Taylor in **Similkameen Symphony.**

Granite Creek

Susan Allison did not enjoy the amenities of a town until many years after her arrival. The first town in the upper Similkameen area was, in fact, Granite Creek, about 15 kilometers northwest of Princeton, site of a gold rush in 1885. That year, Walton Hugh Holmes came from Merritt with a pack train of supplies to the boomtown of Granite Creek, which he describes as "an anthill":

> Several hundred men of all sorts, saddle horses and pack animals, tents on both sides of the river. What a sight! All available space taken up for tents. Campfires everywhere. There was one small cabin built by Mr. Allison for a store, but there were no supplies in it. Only some tin plates and iron knives and forks; no provisions procurable, and they were badly needed. We found our pack trains would be welcome when they arrived. The most of Granite Creek was already staked off for claims. They were only 100 feet long from high water mark to high water mark across the

> creek. There was no Government office to record them, so it was not long before we had to appoint a recorder, a Mr. H. Nicholson, pro tem. till a Government Agent was sent in 1886...By that time Granite Creek was quite a town, all log houses.

At its peak, Granite Creek had a population of about four thousand and offered fifteen premises licenced to serve liquor. It had no church but was visited periodically by preachers from the Presbyterian, Methodist and Anglican churches. In its prime, Granite Creek boasted that it was the biggest town north of San Francisco and east of Winnipeg, a recurring claim of BC boomtowns. But by 1900, Granite Creek was already almost a ghost town.

The Anglican preacher who visited Granite Creek was Henry Irwin, fondly remembered by the miners he served throughout the mining belt of the southern interior -- the west Kootenays, the Boundary country between Rock Creek and Grand Forks, and the upper Similkameen. He was known as **Father Pat** because he was originally from Ireland.

The Emergence of Princeton

The Royal Engineers surveyed a townsite at the confluence of the Similkameen and Tulameen Rivers in 1860. James Douglas, governor of British Columbia, named it Princeton in honour of Edward VII, then Prince of Wales, who was visiting Canada at the time (although he never made to the west) but the emergence of a town at this site was to take another forty years. Until the turn of the century, the economy around Princeton was based on ranching. It was the development of mining activity that spurred the growth of the town.

In the 1860s, John Fall Allison pursued small-scale placer mining for gold. He also found outcroppings of copper, which he later staked. He and other settlers mined their own coal from the banks of the Similkameen and in winter hauled it on sleds over the ice to their homes. It wasn't until 1898, however, with the organization of the Vermilion Forks Mining and Development Company, that the idea of mining coal commercially began. The Company bought the Princeton townsite from John Fall Allison's son-in-law and began selling lots. This scenario is typical of the birth of so many towns in BC. Unlike Europe and eastern North America where towns evolved gradually, towns in the west were "created" out of the wilderness by speculators. The discovery of an exploitable resource is followed by flocks of opportunists who buy up and advertise land and try to sell it at huge profits. A poem published in the *Similkameen Star* 20 January 1906 sums up this spirit of urgent optimism.

> There's no use saying that you can't get cash.
> There's no good delaying for fear of being rash,
> But butt right in and catch on the fly
> One of those big chances that is whizzing by.
> At new town of Welldo where nature has done well
> And the lots will all sell.

Welldo was a townsite near Granite Creek, which never developed into a town. Today, only a handful of people have ever heard of it.

The Vermilion Forks Mining and Development Company secured twelve hundred acres of coal-bearing land adjoining Princeton but commercial coal mining didn't really begin until 1909 with the opening of the Princeton Colliery. At the same time, copper claims were being worked on Copper Mountain and gold was being mined on claims on surrounding creeks. Meanwhile, Princeton underwent a growth spurt. By 1901, its population was 316 and it boasted three hotels, four general stores, three sawmills (indispensable to a growing town), laundries, blacksmiths, lawyers, doctors and -- of course -- real estate offices. And most important as evidence of the town's viability was the existence of a newspaper. The *Similkameen Star* began publication on 31 March 31 1900.

Princeton Community Life

There were few other settlers during the early years of Susan and John Fall Allison's life in the upper Similkameen. Their main contacts were Indians with whom they would have spoken Chinook Jargon. Chinook Jargon, a pidgin trade language constructed from a great variety of Amerindian words, emerged because of the linguistic diversity of western North America. After European contact, Chinook acquired English, French and later Asian and Polynesian words and was the working language in many towns and workplaces, notably in ranch country such as the Similkameen where Indian workers were prevalent.

Indians were part of community celebrations in Princeton from early on. Al Johnston, reminiscing in 1938, remembers the early days:

> Celebrations were always a great rendezvous for the Indians, a feature that persists to the present time, though with nothing like the former ardor. They used to come in with their horses several days ahead, and made a colourful group.

Princeton 1937

The first regular celebration in Princeton was held 1 July 1895 with horse races on the flats by the Allison home. Since 1900 Princeton has had an unbroken line of such Dominion Day (more recently called Canada Day) celebrations. Again, horse races were a vital feature of these celebrations with the klootchmans' race being one of the highlights. "Klootchman" is the Chinook Jargon word for female, and the klootchmen in question were Indian women. The poem **Come and Celebrate**, published in June of 1914, is an invitation in Chinook Jargon to come and join the upcoming Dominion Day celebration.

Princeton Brass Band, 1913. Princeton Museum

Princeton was settled by people from the British Isles who brought with them their habits and culture. During Princeton's early years there existed in England a nation-wide brass band movement. As early as the 1820s, many villages had a band that often participated in organized competitions throughout Britain. Collieries and factories also had their own bands. 1900 saw the revival of a national band festival held annually at the Crystal Palace in London. This coincided with the time Princeton emerged as a town and it was natural for immigrants who settled here to try and recreate what they had left behind in the Old Country. Princeton therefore had to have a brass band. In 1911, "Shrill Bakespeare" in **Ode to Princeton Brass Band** warm-heartedly lampoons the town band that, he says, sounds like an owl hooting which frightens the local marmots back to their nests.

For many years, the Princeton area was home to a significant number of bachelors. Placer miners tended to be single men, and when coal and copper brought single men to work in the mines, many of them congregated in bunkhouses outside town next to the mine where they worked. They lived isolated lives away from the company of women. Imagine their delight, then, when the newspaper announced a "Bachelors' Ball". The sight of so many women must really have gleamed to them "Like a garden of roses and lilies", as is expressed in **To the Princeton Bachelor Maids**.

Hedley

Hedley lies forty kilometers southeast of Princeton at the confluence of Twenty Mile Creek and the Similkameen River. The town exists because of gold discoveries there. The first claims staked on Nickel Plate Mountain above Hedley were those of Edgar Dewd-

Hedley 1940s

ney in 1894 but it wasn't until the turn of the century that the area's riches began to be exploited. In 1897, Peter Scott, C. Johnston and Albert Jacobson climbed Nickel Plate Mountain and found rich showings of gold, and by 1898 nearly every square foot of the mountain had been claimed and registered. Scott staked his claim on behalf of his boss, Robert R. Hedley, manager of Hall Mines smelter in Nelson, after whom the tent camp that quickly emerged was named.

To develop the claims on Nickel Plate Mountain, machinery and equipment were needed. In 1900, the Green Mountain wagon road was built 50 kilometers across the Thompson Plateau to Penticton. This provided a connection to the main line of the CPR at Sicamous via the Shuswap and Okanagan Railway and the CPR's paddlewheeler on Okanagan Lake. At the same time, a settlement for miners and their families was built on top of Nickel Plate Mountain. This marked the beginning of large-scale gold mining and its concomitant boosterism. Until the turn of the century, Hedley had been mostly a tent town, but in 1900, the Hedley City Townsite Company surveyed a street grid for the town. In 1903, school classes began in the Methodist Church and on 19 January 1905 the first issue of the *Hedley Gazette* was published, a sure sign that the town was a going concern.

The Daly Reduction Company of Butte, Montana wanted to build an ore concentrator for the mine at the bottom of the mountain on the Chuchuwayha Indian Reserve #2. M.K. Rodgers, Daly's field man, wrote to Clifford Sifton, the federal Minister of the Interior in Laurier's Liberal government, about releasing land from the Reserve. Sifton contacted A.W. Vowell, Superintendent of Indian Affairs in British Columbia. The Liberals were looking for pre-election support, so on 3 November 1904 the Reserve was trimmed (without consultation or compensation) to make way for the stamp mill and a tailings pond. This incident prompted the publication of **Oh! The Grabbing White Man** in the *Similkameen Star* 22 April 1905. Completion of the mill began fifty years of 24-hour din in Hedley.

Life in Hedley included the typical vicissitudes of everyday life in a small town such as "pushing o'er the Specialist's houses" (outhouses) on Hallowe'en night referred to in **Retribution**. The *Hedley Gazette* ceased publication in August 1917 but gold mining continued on Nickel Plate Mountain until 1955. In the 1960s it resumed with the opening of an open pit mine that closed in the 1980s.

Keremeos

Keremeos lies about 35 kilometers southwest of Hedley on the Similkameen River. The word "Keremeos" comes from "Keremeyeus", which means "creek which cuts through the flats" or "beautiful stream crossing the flats" in the Similkameen dialect of the Okanagan language. In the early1860s the encampment of Indians on this site was invaded by scores of hopefuls panning for gold. In 1860, the Hudson's Bay Company established a post just downstream at the current site of Cawston. Four years later the post was moved upstream and it became the first white habitation at Keremeos. In the mid 1860s, settlers began moving in. At this time, most of British Columbia was crown land, dotted with towns and Indian reservations. To encourage settlement, Governor James Douglas in 1859 issued the Pre-emption Act, whereby settlers could apply to "alienate" crown land into private hands. After staking out his property the settler paid a registration fee of eight shillings. After making the necessary improvements and residency qualification, the settler could purchase the land at ten shillings an acre.

In 1876, Gilbert Malcolm Sproat was appointed to the Joint (federal/provincial) Indian Reserve Commission to allocate Indian reserves in British Columbia. In 1878, he laid out reserves in the lower Similkameen, including a large temporary reserve encompassing Keremeos and what was later to become Cawston. This large reserve was designed to prevent the province from allowing preemptions on Indian land before the final allocation of reserves. But by 1884, the province had sold the best land from the reserve that Sproat had laid out to two ranchers – 555 acres to Mr. Richter and 410 acres to Mr. Cawston, "leaving 381 acres of the most worthless land for the Indians". The Dominion government, under the

British North America Act, was responsible for "Indians and lands reserved for Indians", but the province owned Crown land. This jurisdictional division, combined with the provincial government's attitude towards Indians, made for problems. From 1871, when BC entered confederation, the provincial government's attitude was that Indians "should not be tucked away on reserves [but] should enter the workforce" and become "participating members of civilized society". The wish for integration did not, however, extend to granting Indians the right to preempt land. This left the Indians on reserves they didn't own and which weren't large enough to support them, and with no possibility of actually owning land to support themselves and becoming "participating members of civilized society". At the same time, white people were flooding in and taking over as much land as they could get their hands on.

By 1893, there were sixteen homesteads in the Keremeos area and 1896 saw the first commercial apple orchard. News of the arrival of the Vancouver, Victoria and Eastern Railway from south of the border spurred the creation of the Keremeos Land Company in 1906, which bought 1200 riverside acres. In typical booster fashion, the Company began to lay out a townsite and advertise acreage for sale. To construct a flume to irrigate the acreages, the Company simply trespassed and built on Indian land, ignoring the protests of the Indians.

Settlement and fruit growing flourished in Keremeos' benign climate, celebrated in **Reverie Of An Old Timer**. By the time the railway arrived on 10 July 1907, Keremeos apples were already winning prizes at Provincial exhibitions. By 1910, locals proudly proclaimed in **Canadian National Apple Show** that Keremeos apples shone at the national level.

Coalmont

Coalmont lies about 16 kilometers northwest of Princeton on the Tulameen River. Coal was discovered there in the mid-nineteenth century but it wasn't until the arrival of the railway in 1911 that coal could be shipped out in quantity. Prosperity seemed assured and in 1912 the *Coalmont Courier* was founded and boasted that it was "the largest newspaper in the province outside Kamloops, Vernon and Vancouver." In an ad entitled "Coalmont, the Town of Opportunity", the *Courier* in typical booster fashion, urged prospective buyers of lots to "Take time by the forelock: she has no back hair". The *Courier* ran for only six months, and Princeton's *Similkameen Star* became the main news organ of the area. **The Coalmont Four Hundred**, a parody of Tennyson's "The Charge of the Light Brigade", appeared in the *Courier* in June of 1912. The "Four Hundred" refers to the people who lived in the ritzier part of town.

In 1913, coal mining began higher up the mountain above Coalmont. Production stopped briefly during the First World War but resumed immediately afterwards. A settlement around the mine sprang up and in 1922 was officially named Blakeburn, after William John Blake, President of Coalmont Collieries, and Patrick Burns, of P. Burns & Co. in Vancouver, the vice-president and the other major shareholder of Coalmont Collieries. A three-mile long aerial tramway was completed in 1920 to carry coal to the rail line at Coalmont. Remnants of the tramway can still be found in the woods.

The demise of Coalmont began in the 1930s. On 13 August 1930, known as "Black Wednesday", forty-five miners died in an explosion in the Number 4 mine in Blakeburn. In 1940, the Blakeburn mine closed and Coalmont lost the electricity supplied by the mine's powerhouse. The Second World War extended the life of some of the other mines, but in 1948, coal mining in the area ceased and with it the raison d'être of Coalmont. The last passenger train ran through the town 17 January 1964. Coalmont is now a sparsely populated semi-ghost town without a single shop or restaurant.

Tulameen

Tulameen lies about 16 kilometers northwest of Coalmont on the Tulameen River. The word "Tulameen" comes from an Interior Salish word meaning "red earth". The first Europeans to arrive there were Hudson's Bay traders traveling along the old brigade trails in the mid 19th century. The first settlers were miners from the Granite Creek gold rush, and they created a community named Otter Flats on the shores of Otter Lake. At the turn of the century a proper townsite with a street grid was laid out and in 1901 the name was changed to Tulameen. In 1909, a sawmill opened to supply lumber to fast-growing Coalmont. From 1915, Tulameen was also a regular stopping place of the Kettle Valley Railway for taking on coal and water. The lake, the scenery, the climate and the increased accessibility created by the railway attracted the first recreational visitors.

Tulameen's boom years were the 1920s, starting with the opening of the mine at Blakeburn. "Jay Ell" was the *Princeton Star* correspondent for Coalmont and Tulameen during this time and he contributed many poems to the paper. His 1924 poem, **We Never Hear the Church Bells Ring**, refers to the beach at Otter Lake that attracted the visitors who came by rail. The last verse of Jay Ell's 1926 poem, **The Tulameen Belle**, includes popular colloquial language of the period. It mentions "Captain Kiddo", a movie released in 1917, and one of the movie's catchphrases was "for the love of Mike" – a way to avoid saying "For the love of God". We don't know whether "Captain Kiddo" ever played at the movie theatre in Princeton, but somehow the expression found its way to the Tulameen valley.

Social life in Tulameen, as in all the other communities in the area, included many dances. On Saturday 16 March 1929 there was a St. Patrick's Day dance attended by 150 people at the Britton Hall in Tulameen, which was reported five days later in the *Princeton Star*. People came to the dance from the whole area – Coalmont, Blakeburn, Princeton, Hedley, Keremeos, Merritt, the upper Otter Valley and Manning's Siding. There was no orchestra booked but "there were volunteer players galore so that one was surprised to learn that there were so many talented musicians in the Similkameen district". Typical of almost every dance reported on in the papers until the Second World War, the dance "lasted until daylight". The dance was sponsored by "Mrs. Rabbitt and family". The Rabbitts were a prominent ranching family who had settled in the Tulameen area around the turn of the 20th century. Euphemia Rabbitt is honoured as the "Tulameen Mother" in the poem **St Patrick's Dance** by "Wapella Bill". We don't know who Bill is – perhaps an immigrant to the Tulameen from Wapella, Saskatchewan.

The hills around Tulameen were populated by bachelor prospectors engaged in small-scale placer mining along the creeks and rivers. In 1929, the *Princeton Star* published two poems by Jay Ell -- **Bill and Sam** and **Sam's Supper Soliloquy** -- about a couple of such prospectors. Unlike Bill and Sam, many prospectors lived and often died alone, and the *Similkameen Star* contained frequent stories of prospectors found dead on their claims:

> The body of William Stevenson, an aged placer miner, was found in his tent on the Similkameen River …last Sunday morning. The man had been dead at least a week or ten days and the body was in an advanced stage of decomposition.

The tenacity under primitive and arduous conditions of so many of these bachelor prospectors can be partially explained by their grudging affection for the landscape they live in, as expressed in the Jay Ell poem **Shem, Ham and Japhet**.

Copper Mountain and Allenby

Copper claims were staked on Copper Mountain 16 kilometers south of Princeton as early as 1895 but exploitation of this resource didn't begin until after the turn of the century. In 1913, two mining camps were set up on Copper Mountain and construction began on a mill between Princeton and the mine. The site of this concentrator, about nine kilometers south of Princeton and completed in 1920, was the nucleus of what became the town of Allenby, named after the British field marshal in Egypt and Palestine during the First World War. The *Princeton Star* of 23 May 1919 describes Allenby as "a fine little town equipped with modern community conveniences" populated by families whose children are "growing into husky young British Columbians at an altitude of 4500 feet or better". By 1926, there were 54 houses and 138 employees in the town.

The town of Copper Mountain began as bunkhouses for the workers. In 1928, a fire in one of them burned nine men to death and

Princeton Museum

injured many more. By 1930, Copper Mountain had a community hall and other amenities but, with the price of copper slumping, the mine closed later that year and did not reopen until 1937.

The survival of the towns of Copper Mountain and Allenby depended entirely on the price of copper. In 1944, the town of Copper Mountain was so desperate to survive that it sent a delegation to John Hart, the provincial premier, requesting subsidies to try and prevent the mine from shutting down.

The vulnerability and isolation of mining towns such as Copper Mountain and Allenby elicited a kind of ironic affection such as is expressed in **Ode to Allenby**. The beginning of the second stanza is reminiscent of a popular First World War marching song by Albert Erroll MacNutt about the Union Jack entitled "We'll Never Let the Old Flag Fall" that contains the lines:

"My Country, 'Tis of Thee" we sing,
At the sound of her call, we'll show them all,
We'll never let our old flag fall.

The underground mine at Copper Mountain closed down in 1957, causing the abandonment of the towns of Copper Mountain and Allenby. Some of the houses were sold and transported elsewhere – the streets of Princeton boast many a "miner's cottage" from Allenby. With the exception of a few overgrown foundations and other remnants, the towns of Copper Mountain and Allenby have completely disappeared.

The Copper Mountain mine started up again as an open pit mine in 1960 and closed again in 1996. With rising copper prices, the Copper Mountain Mining Company has recently reopened the mine. But the days of the small, cohesive mining town are over because of improved transportation and the much smaller workforces required for mechanized mining.

The settlement of the Similkameen follows the pattern typical of southern BC's mining belt. A mineral resource is discovered. Claims are staked and shares are sold. Speculators survey town grids and begin selling lots. As mining begins, a town complete with homes, businesses, churches, a school and a newspaper comes into being. The town thrives with the success of the mine. Mineral prices rise and fall and the town's population ebbs and flows. If mineral prices drop too low or the ore is depleted, the town dies and it becomes one of the numerous ghost towns now found throughout southern BC. The Similkameen veers somewhat from this pattern, however, because of agriculture. The first settlers in Princeton were ranchers, and ranching continues today. Keremeos began as a Hudson's Bay Company post but the first wave of settlers ranched and farmed, activities that continue today. Like the Boundary country and the Kootenays to the east, the Similkameen is also riddled with ghost mining towns, but ranching and farming continue to support the people who live here.

A Song of BC

The renegade son of a younger branch
Came out to Vancouver to buy a ranch
And his heart in his breast beat high.
Three hundred sovereigns he had in gold,
An astrakhan coat to confront the cold,
And a glass in his dexter eye.

He selected a farm well stocked with grass,
Three heifers, a pig and a flea-bitten ass,
A bedstead and chairs of silk.
The latest design in mowing machines,
A packet of carrots and kidney beans
And a treatise on 'how to milk'.

But somehow things from there went wrong -
The hens he picked up for the veriest song
Would do nothing else but lay.
The heifers succumbed to a thing called 'bloat',
The pig ate his astrakhan overcoat
And died on that self-same day.

He sat him down with his brain awhirl
And wrote to his uncle, the noble earl,
A letter both strange and sad.
He said he was up to his ears in debts
And the ass and a packet of cigarettes
Were all in the world he had.

By return of post, the noble grim
Had penned this laconic reply to him:
"Dear nephew, it gives me joy
That though of your riches you are bereft,
You have a congenial companion left –
So stick to your pal, my boy."

Similkameen Star, 26 April 1902

In My Dreams

In my dreams last night I wandered
To my dear old English home -
An ivy-covered cottage
Where children ten were born.

Grandpa's clock in a corner stood,
As in days of yore.
The same old easy rocking chair
And worn pictures by the score.

Father and dear mother gone –
But their photos on the wall
Took me back to boyhood days
When I answered to their call.

I saw the old red schoolhouse
Where I went with Lou each day,
Along the hawthorn hedges,
Smelling the new-mown hay.

I kissed a little maiden,
Heard her accepting scream,
And listened to, "I'll tell my ma
If you do that again!"

My dream then was broken
By the autoharp's sweet strain -
I woke surrounded by a pile of logs
On a bank of the Similkameen.

Similkameen Star, 22 February 1902

The Greater Briton In England

A land that is a garden all rose-grown,
Of muffled lawn and odorous lane;
A land of languid rivers and repose,
And ivied green and quiet rain!

An ordered land that broods on yesterday,
Of hearts content with other years,
Of haunted dusks and hills that harbour dreams -
A Country old in time and tears!

But, oh! my heart goes, homesick, back today -
Back to the wide, free prairie's sweep,
Back to the pines that brought the sunset near,
Back where the great white Rockies sleep!

For I am tired of dusk and dream and rose,
Of ghosts and glories dead and gone -
I want the outland trail, the upward sweep,
The New World and the widening dawn!

Similkameen Star, 1 July 1908

Manning Park 1943. The Allan Gill Collection

The Naming of the Similkameen

In the days of Hiawatha,
When we white folks lived in trees,
And for us a new-plucked fig leaf
Made a suit of BVDs.
In those ancient days our river
Followed not its present bed;
Then its course was on the benches,
Benches now high, dry and dead.
Also there was cause to wonder
In the torrent rushing through,
Milk, not water, filled its channel!
- Surely this was something new!
So, when Hiawatha, passing
Westward on his mission bent,
Naming all the lakes and rivers
In his travels as he went.
Hiawatha came to One Mile,
Camped and slept until sunrise;
From his lonely camp on One Mile
Saw this river with surprise.
Searching out a trail from One Mile,
Soon he stood upon the bank;
Gazed upon the mystic river,
Gazing, pondered, stooped and drank.
Drank and smiled and cried "S'milka!",
Smiled to think how pat it came:
'S'milkameenic', 'milk for water'
- Thus our river got its name.

Princeton Star, 12 May 1922

Evening on the Similkameen

One eve I stood on the river's brink,
And looking upward, saw serene above,
The silvery moon, in stilly splendour float.
Light fleecy clouds that scarcely veiled her face
Were drifted upward by the autumn breeze
And as the lacy veil of sun fair bride
O'er her soft shining tresses now upflung,
Revealed to mortal eyes her bright, calm face
Surrounded by attendant sister stars.

But though so stilly bright in heaven, the moon
Her image in the shallow stream beneath
Danced gaily while the gliding water broke
Into a thousand waving ripples.
From out the shallow depths a song arose,
A murmuring song of joy and gladness.
So fair the scene, it seemed a joy to me.
A joy it would have been to gaze forever
Without a thought of the world's pain and care.

While yet I gazed, a wolf's discordant cry
Resounded hideous through the evening air,
Like to a soul in agony and pain,
Recalled me from a trace of mute delight.
I thought of restless ghosts and dying men,
Anon – a pack of fierce mountain wolves,
Loud echoing their scout's unearthly cry,
Rushed panting by, a mad ferocious crowd,
Their shadows in the moonlight hard and cold,
Stretched long and ghastly, flitting through the pines.
Methought 'twas hell broke loose, and all the fiends
Pursuing some poor soul with wild halloos.

And thus for me the witching spell was broke,
The glory of the glorious scene was marr'd.
The moonlight changed from fair to hard and cold,
The river's voice, too, grated harsh and loud.
It told of flood and death and friends bereaved,
And all life's sorrows rushed upon me now
Loosed by the demon wolf's infernal cry.
And wild and weird, the solitary place,
Was now bereft of all its former charms.
Environed by stern mountains, now I felt
Pent in hell's darkest, deepest prison walls,
The ghoulish wolves, in hateful concert now,
Filled the cool air with fiendish, thrilling cries -
Hell's carnival - trembling fled the place,
But awakened thoughts I could not fly.

Similkameen Star, 7 April 1915

Manning Park 1943. The Allan Gill Collection

Similkameen Symphony

Come back to old Similkameen
When summer's on the wing,
Or when the hills in eager green
Wake to the breath of spring.

When violets greet the April morn
And larks sing on the lea,
And little waters, winter born,
Go chattering to the sea.

And when the sun atop the steeps
Attains its full degree,
From out the melting snow bank peeps
The pale anemone.

When from yon shadowy cedared vale
June's lingering light has fled,
The rhododendrons storm the trail
And smother it in red.

The halo of soft summer mist
That hangs about the brow
On frowning Hozameen has kissed
The feet of God, I trow.

'Tis autumn in Similkameen,
And leaves come tumbling down
And Indian Summer tints the green
With amber, red and brown.

The river of ambrosia sups
And hums a silvered tune,
And little smokes go curling up
To veil the sickle moon.

Now winter sternly stills its song,
And decks the dale in white,
But stars the silvered notes prolong
And twinkle through the night.

Come back to old Similkameen -
Who can resist its spell?
A carillon, profound, serene,
From Nature's haunting bells.

Similkameen Star, 3 February 1938

Father Pat

We don't go much on parsons,
Here in the mining belt
Between Rossland and Similkameen,
But there was one we felt
A most uncommon liking for,
You may take my word for that -
The latch string hung outside each door
For good old Father Pat.

He wore the Church of England brand
But didn't bank on creeds;
His way to hearts was not with words,
But helpful, lovin' deeds.
Though we were hard to work upon –
Not readily enticed -
We called him the First Christian
That ever lived - since Christ.

He never peeked at keyholes
Nor fought the cigarette;
He never frowned on lager beer,
Nor games of chance - and yet,
I think that if there is a place
Where good souls get their dues,
They'll find room there for Father Pat,
'Fore preachers you might choose.

He never built no churches,
Nor learned to primp or pose;
His shoes were red and dusty,
And he never wore good clothes;
His manners were just Christian,
Becomin' meek and mild;
And he loved each roughneck miner
Like a mother loves her child.

If one of us was ailin',
He'd take his pack and hike
To that cabin in the mountains
Where illness chanced to strike,
And he never thought of leavin'
Till all was right and well -
And that's why most of us miners won't
Meet Father Pat in hell.

He died: we built a monument
At Rossland, on the hill,
And many sunburned prospectors
Chipped in to pay the bill.
And when I look upon it,
A great big tear starts -
But it's nothing to the monument
He built within our hearts.

Princeton Star, 20 February 1920

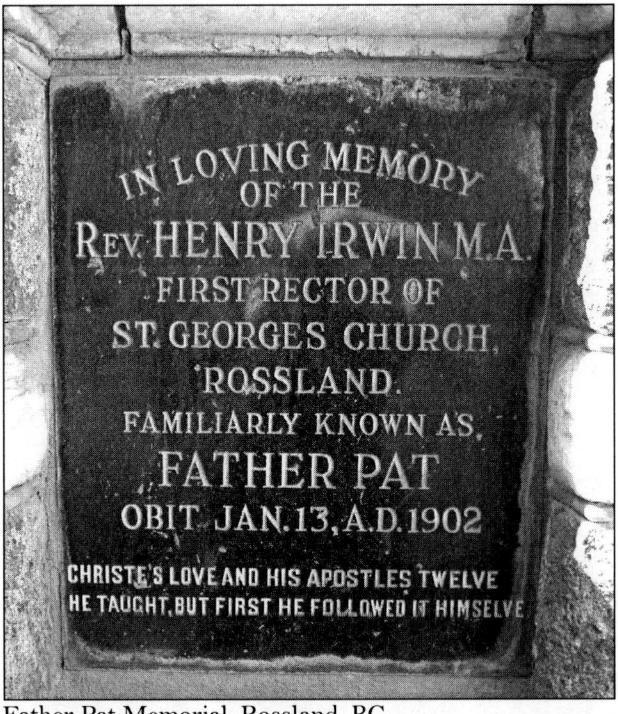

Father Pat Memorial, Rossland, BC

Come And Celebrate

Princeton wawa cupa tillicums chaco.
I,ele mika halo nanitch mika,
Alta mika hehe tumtum-chaco
Konamost konnowa hiash tillicums.
Mamook closh tumtum coupensika,
Hiack chaco shookum man pe kurtan,
Hiack chaco looloo mika klootchman.
Hiack looloo mika papoose,
Scookemet, wacht tenass chinchin,
Wye conawee tooloo hiu hehe,
Kichee connie kurtan, mamook races,
Wacht, shootem target, hiash soupena,
Connie peid konnewa man, klaseta
Midlite cupa sack, klime la peia,
Connie hiack lulu hehe, wye nic!
Hiyu tooloo chickamen, mamook bet,
Klootchman tooloo skookem races, tooloo
Chickamen, iskum hiyu pretty libbon
Istum hiyu pretty icktas nicnic
Telicums chaco cupa Nicola, Kamloops,
Thompson, Osoyoos, Keremeos, Ashnola,
Chechewa, Kunawee hiack chaco hehe.
Kaloo whisky, halloo culthus wawa.
Kounawa straight chaco, chaco,
Mamooh cloch tumtum, Wye selacht.

Similkameen Star, 12 June 1914

A loose translation: Princeton invites all people, great and small, friends and relations to come with laughter in their hearts. There will be horse races. Much money will be won in betting. Racing women will win money and pretty ribbons to make many beautiful things. People will be coming from Nicola, Kamloops, Thompson, Osoyoos, Keremeos and Ashnola. There will be laughter and whisky and no worthless talk. So come, come, we invite you from the heart.

Ode to Princeton Brass Band: a Paroxysm in Several Fitts

Fitt Ye First

What are those fearsome sounds that do assail mine ears?
More awesome that the coyote's howl, that fills my soul with fear,
Is it a carpet that they beat, or doth some tortured soul
Seek to be free from earthly pain, to gain a heavenly goal?

Fitt Ye Second

Does mother hush her infant to slumber's sweet repose
By threats of dissolution from frantic Indian foes?
Swooped from some rocky fastness, with sound of tom-tom shrill,
That shrieks from out the mountains and echoes from the hill.

Fitt Ye Third

But no, from out thy sanctum proceeds the awful dirge,
Surely thy sins must grievous be to warrant such a scourge?
Music, we know, hath power to soothe the savage breast,
But is THAT music which I hear that makes my soul opprest?

The Answer

Silence to thee, O scoffer, who prates about thy soul,
Know only that by travail we may obtain our goal.
The fiercesome sounds thou hearest will echo through the land
In sweet and tuneful melody, from Princeton's First Brass Band.

Go to it, noble drumster, let B flat cornet sound,
Mark how the startled hopper comes bounding from the ground.
The marmot seeks his rocky nest, the owl of ill repute,
Welcomes a lusty rival with many a distant hoot.

Here's luck to all the joiners, come with thy sackbut gay;
And blow with all thy might and main, to make a festal day.

Similkameen Star, 28 June 1911

To the Princeton Bachelor Maids

Some were blonde, others brunette,
Not one will we ever forget.
Each fairer and more lovely than the other, it seemed
Like a garden of roses and lilies they gleamed,
Dainty, debonair and most bewitching,
Were these jolly bachelor maids of Princeton.

There were Nellie and Naomi, Hazel and Marie,
Anna, Mabel and Polly, all fair to see;
'Sunshine' and Mary, Edna and Gladys,
Frances, Annie and Ada, all there to entrance us.
Lillian and Louise, Mildred and Lizzie,
Katy, Anna and Ada, by now
We are distractingly dizzy,
Our brains are in a whirl
With these bachelor girls.
But pray tell us, how is it
With your wit and your wiles,
Your charms and your smiles,
How have you ever kept single?

Like fairies you dance,
Every one you entrance,
And many a heart you make tingle.
With your laughing eyes,
And your rosy cheeks,
Your winning smiles
And your gracious ways,
You could share the throne with any king.
Here's hoping you will some day.

But bachelor maids you need not be,
For there are bachelor boys that think as me.
So if you remain it will be your own wish,
And instead of Mrs. you keep it a Miss.

But which ever you choose, may you never regret,
And your kindness to us we will not soon forget.
Good managers, good cooks, success of your balls
Proves you are capable and clever each one and all.
As hostesses you are supreme,
Our hats are off to each bachelor queen.

Similkameen Star, 28 May 1915

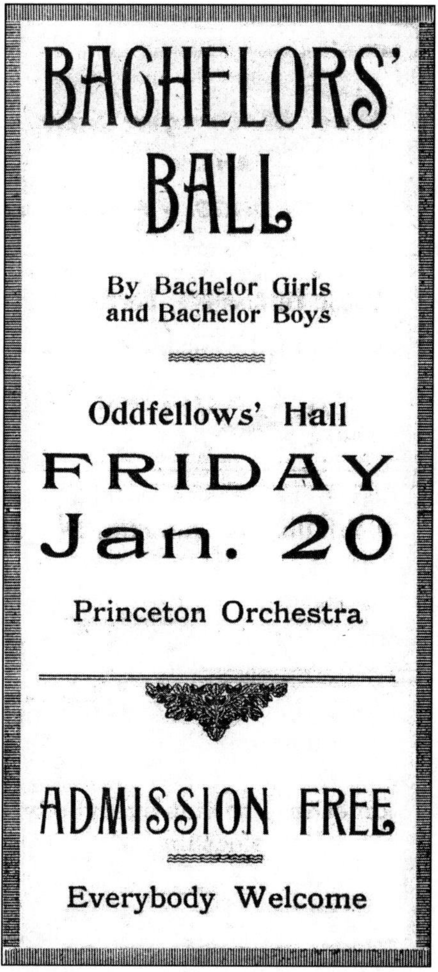

Similkameen Star, 13 January 1922

Oh! the Grabbing White Man

On the death of Cos-a-tas-ket (Pinto), medicine man to the Chuchuwayhas tribe near Hedley, a rumour went out that having no male heir, the old man's land was public property and therefore jumpable. Hardly was the old man's remains lowered to that abode where white and red man alike must go than several bold white men staked that portion of the late owner's reserve. An invocation to the spirit of the deceased was, therefore, made as follows:

Spirit of Cos-a-tas-ket, why
Do white men stake the fair domain
So lately held by you on earth?
Your grandson, P'lix, ploughs up the same.
Tell him and others of your race
The error of the sly pale face!

The spirit being thus invoked, answereth:

Ankate nika stop copa mika
Hiu white man cutun stop kopa nika field
Pe white man halo potlach chikamun
Yaka cutun kapswaller nika tipsum
Kopet hay pe halo chikamun stop kopa nika
Alta nika mamloose, white man kapswaller nika illahie.

Karqua nika wawa Cos-a-tas-ket :

"Son of my son and Indian brothers all,
Before the 'white' can push thy claims aside,
There'll have to be some 'good old summer time'
And Pinto's wife again shall be a bride."

Similkameen Star, 22 April 1905

Retribution

Whose were those wry and sheepish faces
That followed the Police with lagging paces?
Who were the lads whose ire was plain
As they tagged the Law up each back lane?

They were the lads who, in yesteryear,
Of Hallowe'en fun had had their share.
They, it was, who'd been given the blame
While the younger boys had had the game

Of pushing o'er the Specialist's houses.
("The darned unmentionable little louses")
And people smiled at their rank debasement
As over each hole they made replacement.

MORAL
As you take your fun so shall you pay,
If not now, in a later day.
It does no good to rant or weep
Or as ye sow, so shall ye reap.

Similkameen Star, 14 November 1940

Manning Park 1943. The Allan Gill Collection

Reverie Of An Old Timer

O, it was cold in Princeton,
It was 51 below;
Hedley, she marked 40,
Besides three feet of snow.

Chorus
The sun shines in the valley
And makes a warm glow,
For it ne'er gets down to zero
In Keremeos below.

The apples here grow quite large
And I know will pay in time,
While the peaches are the finest
I have seen in any clime.

The pumpkin, squash and melon
Here in profusion grow,
And remind me of old Kentucky
Some forty years ago.

And along those sunny foothills
Where the thousands cattle roam,
Neath those majestic mountains
Higher than Washington's great Dome.

And when comes the coming Winter
They feed among the glades,
In the Similkameen valley
That lies east of the Cascades.

While the sun shines in the valley
And makes a warm glow,
It ne'er gets down to zero
In Keremeos below.

Hedley Gazette, 18 April 1907

Canadian National Apple Show

If you want to see the banner booth of all the Apple Show,
Just come and we will tell you where you surely ought to go;
Where the apples red and golden are spread out in grand array
And when you stand before that booth it's hard to get away.
There's a lady in the question, too, who truly is the queen
Of the District represented - the fair Similkameen -
And of all the fruit exhibits at this First Apple Show,
Keremeos has the best - so that's the place to go
To see the orchard beauties arranged with taste so keen,
The pride of Keremeos - in the fair Similkameen.

Hedley Gazette, 1 December 1910

Princeton 1912. Princeton Museum

The Coalmont Four Hundred

Satire to right of them,
Rude jest ahead of them,
The common herd behind them,
Volleyed and thundered:
Scorned they the shot and shell
(Though one can never tell
If any of it got home to them),
As straight through the Valley of Coalmont
Strode the 'Four Hundred'.

Coalmont Courier, 17 June 1912

We Never Hear The Church Bells Ring

We never hear the church bells ring,
Nor yet a sexton see;
We never hear the church choir sing,
No church nor choir have we.

Yet though we cannot join a choir,
Nor hear a parson preach,
We like to visit and admire
The belles upon the beach.

For on a summer Sunday morn,
There can be heard and seen
The sweetest belles to beach adorn -
The belles of Tulameen.

Princeton Star, 7 August 1924

Rock drilling contest, Dominion Day 1913 at Princeton. Princeton Museum

The Tulameen Belle

I loved her so, it could not be
That love like mine had ever been;
She was the fairest of the fair,
The sweetest girl in Tulameen.

I loved her for her sparkling eye,
I loved her for her winning way,
I cannot tell the reason why,
But yet, I knew not what to say.

I stood and stammered for a time
And no doubt looked just like a fool,
Till I bethought me of a rhyme
That I had learned when I went to school.

I sprung it while I held her hand
And gazed into her azure eyes,
I thought I'd reached the happy land,
But, oh my! what a great surprise.

"The rose is red, the violets blue,
The honey's sweet and so are you".

And then my darling Mary Blend
Said, "Kiddo, you have said enough,
And if you want to be my friend,
For love o' Mike, cut out that stuff."

Princeton Star, 3 December 1926

St Patrick's Dance

The Bunnies had a dance last night,
All sporting on the green;
Shamrock and clover leaves,
Predominate the scene.

The crowd was very large,
The floor was extra slick;
The girls, they all were there;
Each man, his choice to pick.

The music was supreme,
The dancers, just the same;
All with a different 'hop',
Which makes other dances tame.

On the program of the evening
Came a dance that's full of pep;
The 'Tulameen' concoction,
The famous 'Brownie' step.

Old timers, they were there,
Real men and women they;
From near and far they came,
To help the youngsters play.

To snare Bunnies seems a shame,
But boys, you'd better step;
There's a live trapper in the game,
And he's making quite a rep.

Now for that sumptuous supper,
Sandwiches and cakes galore;
And steaming fragrant coffee,
A second cup, and more.

To several we give credit,
For the good time given all;
But foremost on the list,
Is the hostess of the ball.

'Tulameen Mother' she is called
By many who know her well;
And she lives up to her name,
As true as the old church bell.

I don't belong to the mountains,
But since I came here,
I've met some good-hearted people
Who deserve the best of cheer.

Princeton Star, 28 March 1929

Bill And Sam

Old Bill and Sam, they shared a shack
Not far from Tulameen.
Sam was the cook, and had the knack
To keep Bill's belt from getting slack,
Though Bill was rather lean.

Bill was inclined to sit and fret
When feeling kind o' blue,
And oftentimes he'd doze, and let
The day go by, and quite forget
That he had chores to do.

Said Bill to Sam, "I wish I had
A half a million beans.
I'd pack my grip and glam my wad
And beat it out of here, by Dad,
And head for other scenes."

Said Sam to Bill, "I seldom wish -
It never does much good,
For wishing never caught a fish,
Nor boiled a spud, or washed a dish,
But - I wish you'd chop some wood."

Princeton Star, 18 May 1923

Sam's Supper Soliloquy

I'm gettin' tired of hearing old Bill curse,
For day by day he's gettin' worse and worse;
There's nothing seems to suit him now at all;
When spring comes round, he wishes it was fall.
And if the fall were here he'd still complain,
And wish it was the summer time again.
He darns the hills, the rivers, trees and rocks;
He darns 'most everything - except his socks.
Our old log shack don't suit him any more,
And any little job's a tiresome chore.
The grub don't taste the way it used to do;
Potatoes are the worst that ever grew.
He never tackled meat so awfully tough,
The coffee that I make isn't good enough,
The bread's too fresh or else it is too stale.
He thinks that he'd be better fed in jail;
And so, from day to day I hear him moan,
Until I often wish I lived alone.

It don't seem long since first we took the trail,
And yet it's plain to see Bill's gettin' frail;
His movements now are mostly very slow,
Compared to what they were ten years ago.
And maybe, after all, I'm some to blame.
My cooking may not be so good's I claim;
The meat sure has been rather tough of late,
The spuds are not the best I ever ate.
I've seen the day when I'd bake better bread;
So maybe it is true, Bill's not well fed.
Ah well! I guess I've got it all complete.
"Hey Bill! The supper's ready; come and eat."

Similkameen Star, 15 June 1923

Shem, Ham and Japhet

Said Shem, "I wish that I could go
To some far Southern clime,
Where luscious fruits and flowers grow,
With sunshine all the time."

Said Ham, "I'd gladly emigrate
To Florida with you;
But memories make me meditate
Upon the thought: this sunshine state
Is moonshine too."

Said Japhet, "To the longing eyes,
The far-off fields look green,
To me 'twould seem a safe surmise
Though you two were in Paradise,
You'd wail for Tulameen."

Princeton Star, 9 February 1923

General store, Hedley, 1920s

Ode to Allenby

Fair Allenby! Where children fight,
Cats do scratch, and the neighbours might!
The grown-ups walk around and frown,
Because it is five miles from town.

Fair Allenby! Of thee we sing!
No gas, no coupons, and no ping!
The car is finally all run down,
And we're just five little miles from town.

Fair Allenby! Oh when we leave,
It is with tears upon our sleeve,
Thinking of that road going down,
And hoofing it up, five miles from town!

Fair Allenby! We think of thee,
When we're in Princeton drinking tea!
And shopping for gum, girdle, and gown,
Trying to forget the five miles from town.

Fair Allenby! It is with joy,
That we behold thee and thine alloy!
With blistered heels and bursting crown,
Stumbling back, five miles from town!

The Similkameen Star, 2 August 1945

Trestle on Copper Mountain Spur. Princeton Museum

Chapter 3: Boosterism

The establishment of towns in the Similkameen valley at the turn of the century took place at a time of expansion and economic growth throughout western North America. Resource extraction in the hinterlands saw the emergence of many new towns. The sense that the prosperity would go on forever gave rise to a civic identity of towns as cities-in-waiting -- many of the mining towns that mushroomed in BC's wilderness boasted that they were the "biggest settlement north of San Francisco and west of Winnipeg". Some even incorporated as cities when their population numbered only in the hundreds. The assumption was that cities could be made by hardworking, optimistic visionaries. These people were known as boosters and their ethos suffused the growth of western North America at the turn of the century.

Donald Wetherell sums up the tenets of boosterism:

> Its dreams of self-help and initiative, its promise to allow the individual to cast his own fate, its pledge of social acceptance for those who supported its tenets, its belief in the importance of community cohesiveness and positive thinking to promote individual success and its habitual blurring of the lines between private interests and those of the community created the intellectual and political framework of town life and shaped and justified its business and social life. . . .

A "booster" is someone who believes in the present and future success of their town and says only positive things about it. A booster works hard and is rewarded for his labours by prosperity. The opposite of a booster is a "knocker" or a "flopper", someone who doesn't work hard, who is not rewarded with prosperity and who often pooh-pooh's the booster. The booster resents the knocker and sees him as an obstacle to progress and economic growth. **Be a Man: to the Knockers and Floppers**, for example, tells the knocker not to "stand in the way of the brave ones", i.e., the boosters. The poem was submitted to the *Similkameen Star* by Tom Gorman of Cold Creek, Similkameen, and was obviously popular at the time, since it appeared under the title "Get Out and Hustle" in the *Grey River Argus* in New Zealand on the same day as it was published in the *Star*. The poem is typical of many poems and articles on this topic published around the turn of the century both in Princeton and throughout settler societies in western North America, Australia, New Zealand and South Africa.

Boosterism functioned as a force of social cohesion whereby civic identity was constructed in terms of economic growth. The heyday of boosterism in the early 1900s was thus a time of the formation of local boards of trade -- Princeton's was established in 1903. Boosterism gave ambitious people reason to settle in a town and defined citizenship and appropriate civic behaviour. The poem **Buy At Home**, published in the *Hedley Gazette* in 1915, recommends one form of appropriate civic behaviour. In this atmosphere it was easy to blur the line between public and private interests, especially since the town movers and shakers were the business people. C.V. Prosser owned a harness and shoe repair shop in Princeton in the 1920s. He ran regular advertisements in the *Princeton Star* and also wrote a poem extolling the virtues of his shop. Since economic growth was the ethos of the town, there was no perceived conflict of interest when Prosser submitted and the newspaper published his poem, **Where to Buy, What to Buy, and Why**.

At the core of boosterism is the idea that what is good for business is good for the town and what is good for the town is good for everyone in it. Boosters believe in the trickle-down theory of wealth distribution. Those who generate the wealth are the boosters and those to whom it trickles down are presumably the have-nots in the community whose existence the boosters don't understand, because the boosters' code of self-reliance makes them blind to class differences. In fact, the booster in **It Isn't your Town – It's You** believes that there will be no have-nots if "everybody works and nobody shirks". This poem by R.W. Glever was widely published in American newspapers at the time.

Together with hard work comes the necessity of continually boosting your town. The author of **Be a Booster** implores the reader to "just keep that horn a-blowin'" or else things might "be in a sorry plight" and the booster in **His Middle Name** (by Kearey Hub) "just smiles and smiles and smiles when things are going bad". Both these poems were also widely published in American newspapers in the early decades of the 20th century. Boosterism thus resembles a nascent religion where all converts have to believe desperately together or else the whole edifice crumbles.

Boosterism also resembles the stock market, where rises and falls in stock depend largely on investor confidence. For a town to be viable, it needs a resource base. Once a resource base has been identified, the land speculators move in and extol the limitless future of the resource thus guaranteeing the future of the town. To attract population, the town needs to have services and community facilities for the people buying lots. The viability of a town depends on the existence of such things as stores, schools, churches, service clubs, sports teams and a newspaper. The presence of these attracts and keeps town population. It also creates confidence, which in turn creates wealth for the land speculators and business people -- the boosters.

During their initial growth spurts, western boomtowns typically incorporated very quickly. The promoters and speculators sought town status because it offered greater borrowing power. This provided funding for the development of civic services, which would in turn attract population and investment. It also allowed the leading business people to be elected to town council and thus wield political as well as economic power. The mining boomtowns of the Boundary and Kootenay regions east of Princeton incorporated almost as soon as they were built -- Greenwood, Rossland and Nelson, for example, in 1897 and Kaslo in 1893. Princeton was a noticeable exception to this rule. It was first surveyed in 1860, emerged as a town at the turn of the century but did not incorporate until 1951.

Laurie Currie in *Princeton 120 Years* argued that business people opposed Princeton's incorporation because they believed it would raise taxes. "Solid citizens came to Princeton, stayed only a short time, then left; those who did stay became so firmly entrenched that they virtually controlled the economy of the community". In 1902, the Vermilion Forks Mining and Development Company owned 320 acres at the confluence of the Similkameen and Tulameen Rivers where it laid out Princeton's street grid. In 1909, this company was reorganized as the Princeton Coal and Land Company with Ernest Waterman as local Director. At this time Waterman ran full-page ads in almost every issue of the *Similkameen Star* extolling the economic advantages and beauties of Princeton. Waterman was therefore one of Princeton's leading "solid citizens" who "controlled the economy of the community" but he must also have been a stumbling block to incorporation. It was finally the son of a hard-rock miner, Isaac Plecash, who provided the necessary leadership to bring about incorporation.

The First World War was a watershed throughout western society. The 19th and early 20th centuries saw huge social and technological changes with the establishment of public education systems, the emergence of unions, the struggles for women's suffrage and the exploration and colonization of uncharted territory. The development of railways and steamships revolutionized the transport of people and freight. It was a time of unbridled optimism where anything seemed possible. The First World War put a sudden end to this epoch. A generation of young men from Europe and North America was butchered and the technological advances designed to make life better were now bent to death and destruction. After such a blow it was no longer possible to see the world through the optimistic eyes of the booster.

The cataclysm of the First World War and the economic hardship that followed undermined the booster belief in the ability of the individual to control his own fate. Positive thinking and economic growth could no longer be forces of community cohesion. In fact, no new towns were established in southern BC during this period and many already established had shrunk to near non-existence or had become ghost towns. The citizens of those surviving towns had to look elsewhere for civic identity. Now, instead of yearning to grow, towns began to celebrate their social stability and friendliness, qualities that cities were thought to lack. In **Princeton Friendship**, for example, the poet, W.H. Haynes of Princeton, speaks of how "Princeton, small but sound" offered him "true friendship".

Another focus of identity for townspeople was the beauties of nature surrounding them. Early twentieth century poetry collections are full of odes to nature as well as poems, by such luminaries as Rudyard Kipling and Walter de la Mare in Britain, and Henry Lawson and A.B. "Banjo" Paterson in Australia, about the longing of cramped urban dwellers for the wide-open spaces. Towns in the west could boast to eastern cities of their natural beauty as well as of the commonly-found camaraderie of new towns. Here, there was no rat race to dehumanize people and alienate them from one another. After the First World War, towns in the west exchanged their boosterism for the small-town values of friendliness and a sense of community. The cliché of western friendliness is epitomized in a poem by the American turn of the century poet, Arthur Chapman, published in the *Similkameen Star* in 1920 that begins:

> Out where the handclasp's a little stronger,
> Out where a smile dwells a little longer,
> That's where the west begins.

Towns in the west embraced this version of themselves, instead of emulating cities, felt morally superior to them. "How Some Easterners Regard Us", written from the point of view of an easterner and published in the *Similkameen Star* in 1901, contains a plethora of patronizing clichés about the west but its eastern narrator ends by saying:

And yet we love those ratty cranks,
Out West,
We get the gold to fill our banks,
Out West,
They dig it up in every yard,
And that is why we try so hard
To hold them in our high regard,
Out West.

Boosterism was not an exclusively western phenomenon, but during the expansion of the Canadian and American West around the turn of the century, it became epidemic, as small town boosters made extravagant predictions for their settlement in the hope of attracting more residents and, not coincidentally, inflating real estate prices. The convulsion of the First World War and the ensuing economic uncertainly spelled disaster for some western towns, and a few of them disappeared entirely. Those that survived shifted their stance from one of limitless growth to one of community cohesion and quality of life.

Bridge St. in Princeton, 1928. Princeton Museum

Be a Man! To the Knockers and Floppers

This world is a world of sore trials at best -
We've all got our crosses to bear;
And if in the battle your rubbery knees
Are shaking with fear in your pants,
Don't stand in the way of the braver ones, please -
Make a sneak and give others a chance.

Don't sit in the dumps with a scowl on your face
And see the procession go by,
Catch step with the boosters and hold to their pace
And step mighty sassy and high.
If lacking in nerve or of sand in your craw,
Too shiftless to onward advance,
Don't try to play even by swinging your jaw -
Make a sneak and give others a chance.

Don't lazy around with despair in your eyes
And grumble and growl at your luck,
For knocking and swearing won't help you to rise
You've got to have ginger and pluck:
If lacking in nerve to stay in with the play,
Don't give us a gruff song and dance,
But stir your old stumps and get out of the way -
Make a sneak and give others a chance.

Similkameen Star, 14 May 1904

Overlooking Princeton, 1943. The circle indicates the Three Brothers peaks. The Allan Gill Collection

Where To Buy, What To Buy, And Why

Let me whisper to you in these lines I will say,
When you want a good harness, you'll find it will pay
To call upon Prosser and make your wants known,
And buy something nice that you'll be proud to own.

Other tradesmen may kick at the prices as I make him,
But let 'em kick on for we're here to teach 'em
That we're out for business and will keep prices down;
And they may as well bear it and grin as to frown.

All I want is a grub-stake and suit of old clothes,
Hat, shoes and socks and a wipe for my nose;
Wealth is no object, and I don't care a clam,
Just to show what a plunger I am.

What I carry is harness, whips, lap robes and lines,
Auto mats and horse collars, leather cuffs and horse blinds,
Horse hobbles, dog collars, feed bags, hames and tugs;
Horse notions of all kinds for horses or plugs.

Auto tops I can order, curtains I make,
Horse blankets I carry and they are no fake,
Fixings of all kinds I have in my store,
Web bridles and halters and a thousand things more.

So bring me your trade and a dollar or two.
I'll do your work cheap. Now the deal's up to you;
Be wise, buy your harness and such things from me
Honest old Prosser of Princeton, BC.

Princeton Star, 26 May 1922

Buy at Home

When you want to help your town, buy at home.
When you want shoes, hat or gown, buy at home.
Never mind what 'tis you need - canned goods, collars, chicken feed,
Frame this phrase up for your creed - buy at home.

Other folks may buy by mail, buy at home.
Help the home store to a sale, buy at home.
Every dollar sent away means a dollar less to pay,
What is owed right here today - buy at home.

Are you for your town or not? Buy at home.
Cheaper elsewhere? Tommyrot - buy at home.
Home store qualities are true, home store merchants work for you.
This much then you ought to do - buy at home.

Hedley Gazette, 28 October 1915

Similkameen Star 24 February 1922

It Isn't Your Town – It's You

If you want to live in the kind of town
Like the kind of a town you like,
You needn't slip your clothes in a grip
And start on a long, long hike.
You'll only find what you left behind,
For there's nothing that's really new.
It's a knock at yourself when you knock your town.
It isn't your town – it's you.

Real towns are not made of men afraid
Lest somebody else gets ahead.
When everybody works and nobody shirks
You can raise a town from the dead.
And if, while you make your personal stake,
Your neighbor can make one too,
Your town will be what you want to see.
It isn't your town – it's YOU.

Similkameen Star, 18 December 1914

KEEP YOUR EYES ON

CAMP HEDLEY

WATCH IT GROW

It is destined to be the Greatest Gold Mining Camp in Canada.

Money invested in Hedley Town Property now will bring you Big Returns in a Few Months

Buy Now; Don't Put It Off as the Price is Going Up.

For Full Information Write or Call on

THE HEDLEY CITY TOWNSITE COMPAPY, Ltd.,

F. H. French, Secretary and Manager - HEDLEY, B.C.

Similkameen Star 20 June 1910

Be A Booster

Do you know there's lots 'o people
Settin' round in every town,
Growlin' like a broody chicken,
Knockin' every good thing down?
Don't you be that kind 'o cattle,
'Cause they ain't no use on earth,
You just be a booster rooster,
Crow and boost for all you're worth.

If your town needs boostin', boost 'er;
Don't hold back and wait to see.
If some other fella's willin' –
Sail right in, this country's free.
No one's got a mortgage on it,
It's just yours as much as his,
If your town is shy on boosters,
You get in the boostin' biz.

If things just don't seem to suit you
And the world seems kinder wrong,
What's the matter with a-boostin'
Just to help the thing along?
'Cause if things should stop again
We'd be in a sorry plight;
You just keep that horn a-blowin',
Boost 'er up with all your might.

If you know some feller's failin's,
Just forget 'em, 'cause you know
That same feller's got some good points,
Them's the ones you want to show.
'Cast your loaves out on the waters,
They'll come back's a sayin' true,
Maybe, too, they'll come back 'buttered'
When some feller boosts for you.

Similkameen Star, 5 June 1912

His Middle Name

He isn't handsome - far from that, as manly beauty goes;
He doesn't sport the latest hat or up-to-date clothes.
And yet he is more popular than all the blooming roost;
And everybody likes him, for his middle name is BOOST.

He doesn't wear the latest styles or know the latest fad;
But he just smiles and smiles and smiles when things are going bad.
He talks a lot, when rain clouds pour, of crops they have produced ;
He sees their silver lining, for his middle name is BOOST.

He makes no million bucks a year, and yet he has enough;
His charity is giving cheer when things are looking tough.
Of friends he owns a plenty, more than money has induced;
Yep, everybody likes him, for his middle name is BOOST.

Get out yourself and boost a bit and jolly folks along,
For knocking never makes a hit when things are breaking wrong.
If you should hear a kicker roar, just bump him off the roost
And show the folks you're plugging, for your middle name is BOOST.

Similkameen Star, 5 June 1914

Princeton Friendship

It was a dull November morn
When first I hit this town;
And I said, "I cannot stand this burg,"
As I wandered all around.
But fate had sent me on my quest,
And Princeton, small but sound,
Had claimed another settler
Who'd found a stamping ground.

The days were long and dreary
And the evenings lonesome, too;
And I shivered in my little room,
And daily grew more blue.
But soon I found good friendship,
Then the days were not so slow,
When I gathered 'round their fireplace
With no other place to go.

So they in friendship met me
And I know they're sound and true;
And many and many an evening
I've enjoyed with naught to rue.
But the coalmine calls us, fellows,
And morning comes too soon;
So I'd leave their cheerful home life
And walked home by the moon.

If they're down and out and weary,
I'll hope I'll be on hand
To show appreciation in our adopted land.
True friendship doesn't waver
With every word, it's true.
It's no alloy - but solid gold,
And you'll find but very few.

I'm still in dear old Princeton;
The town would be naught to me
If there wasn't a little friendship;
I'd far, far rather be
In a place where people gather
And they care not what they say;
Such are your great big cities,
Where friendship holds no sway.

Princeton Star, 26 December 1919

Government Head-quarters For the Similkameen District.

BEAUTIFULLY SITUATED at the Forks of the Similkameen and Tulameen Rivers. The BUSINESS CENTRE for the following Mining Camps:— Copper Mountain Kennedy Mountain, Friday, Boulder and Granite Creeks, Summit, Roche River, Upper Tulameen and Aspen Grove

FINE CLIMATE
AND PURE WATER
ENORMOUS AGRICULTURAL AREA TO DRAW FROM

Send for Map and Price List to

ERNEST WATERMAN,

Resident Manager VERMILION FORKS MINING AND DEVELOPMENT CO.

Similkameen Star 10 August 1901

Chapter 4: The Weekly Press

Mining towns' life stories are identical in outline, and only the details are unique. First, there are prospectors, looking for good "showings" of ore. On finding them, they stake the area. Mines need capital, something almost never possessed by prospectors, and so the mining claims are sold to mining companies. Where prospects are good, a mine is dug. This requires workers, who need housing, food, and transport to and from the mine. The ore from the mine has to be milled, refined and smelted. This requires transportation, most conveniently a railway. A feature of this microeconomy are the businessmen who move to satisfy those needs, and who also need a secure town to make it worth their while to establish themselves. A worker can pack his tools and move on when the mine is played out, but the grocer, the printer, and the publican have capital tied up. Thus the businessmen become boosters, to try to ensure that the town has some permanence.

The newspaper holds a central role in boosting. The owner and editor share in both the positive and negative drives of boosting – more businesses means more advertising revenue, and the owner has significant capital invested in the town, through owing a printing press. The newspaper comes out on a regular schedule, and whether there is news or no, must contain something for the reader. The editor was in those days by and large an independent businessman, sometimes answerable only to the owner (which he may also have been). He was free to say what he liked, subject of course to his readership. He brought to the task his printing skills and his wide general knowledge, and he had to know and satisfy the working-class tastes of his subscribers. The Princeton editor, for example, noted in April 1908 that

> (T)he miners of Hedley have organized a union and are now connected with the Western Federation of Miners. The new union starts off with a large membership, and the *Star* editor, who is a Union man, wishes the Hedley miners every success.

This was an unusual position for an editor, whose main concern was finding enough advertisements to make the paper pay – and a sympathy for unions oftentimes would have the reverse effect. But in a town whose population was mostly miners, the editor has to play both sides of the fence.

The paper typically consisted of local ads, many of a legal nature (timber licences, claim stakes and the like); regional or national ads (where the town had close enough connection with a city); local news, extending to the territory of the next town; some provincial news relevant to the interior; important national news, including war questions; very occasionally, cartoons; and "filler" – "believe it or not" type pieces, and poems and songs, sometimes drawn from national or international resources (such as established poets like Alfred Tennyson or Christina Rossetti), sometimes from popular poets (Edgar Guest, Eugene Field, S.E. Kiser, James Russell Lower, James Whitcomb Riley, or Ella Wheeler Wilcox), and much more often, from local authors.

It is these last who concern us, and whose work we believe is worth examining to reflect on life lived locally. The weekly papers in whose pages their pieces appeared are the *Similkameen Star/Princeton Star* (1900-1945), the *Hedley Gazette* (1905-1917), and the *Coalmont Courier* (1912).

The first of these is the *Similkameen Star.* Its first issue appeared 31 March 1900, and it was published by J. Anderson. The paper itself was financed by A.E. Howse, a local storeowner and rancher. Anderson was succeeded by B. Stone Kennedy, who ran it for less than a year; J.M. Wright, Robert Lowery (who was the owner over the period of the First World War and hired F.J. Smyth as editor for part of the period), R.J. McDougall (with L. Pilkington as manager), George E. French, Joe A. Brown, Dave Taylor and Dr. John Goodfellow (who saw the paper through the Second World War). Dave Taylor took it back over in 1946 on his return from Europe, but after 1950 the paper began to publish only irregularly. The paper was titled the *Similkameen Star* throughout, except for a name change to *Princeton Star* from 1918 to 1934.

Though the role of editor was a crucial one in a small town, it is curious that only three of these editors made much of a name for himself; Lowery, a newspaper man of great experience, mostly in the Kootenays, where over the course of 20-odd years he edited or created some 22 papers; Dave Taylor, who arrived in Princeton in 1927 and who held the job the longest; and Dr. John C. Goodfellow, the first historian of the Similkameen valley and a local clergyman.

The *Hedley Gazette* (1905-1917) was born and died under one owner and editor, "Major" Ainsley McGraw. The *Coalmont Courier* (1912), owned by A.E. Howse and edited by E.N. Clark, began publication in May of 1912. Due to transportation delays, the newsprint did not arrive in time for printing the first issue so Clark used brown wrapping paper donated by local businessmen. The first page contained the lament, **Soliloquy on the Procrastination of Railroads**. The *Courier* had a life of only six months. "One by one," as Dave Taylor reported in 1937, "they gave up the ghost and were incorporated with the *Star*".

Common to all newspapers is the demand for ads. Advertisements pay for paper and ink, distribution and salaries – the cost of the Princeton paper to subscribers ($2 a year from the paper's founding to at least 1951) never covered more than a small fraction of the costs. To sell ad space required a hustling salesman, with humour and gumption and gall.

Two pieces promote the need for advertising. The first appears to be by M.L. Corey, with the Indiana Hardware Association. His piece **He Does Not Advertise**, on the need to advertise, appeared in the *Similkameen Star* 1 December 1916 and was quickly copied throughout the English-speaking world in the years before the First World War. The second, **A Wise Geezer**, is from the same period and was likewise copied across North America.

To get ads, the paper must demonstrate that it has readers, and readers need news. Most southern interior papers in the early years of the century were one-man operations and it was thus physically impossible (especially in the days before telephones) to gather all the news of the catchment area of the paper. Two pieces, **Send It In** (1922) and **The Editor's Plea** (1941) reflect the need for a constant stream of local news – births, marriages, deaths, strikes, accidents, school reports – the paper's maw was insatiable. "Stringers" (freelance journalists who contribute items on an ongoing basis and are paid by the piece) from outlying towns were smiled upon by editors, and Princeton had a few, the most creative of them being "Jay Ell" of Coalmont, a fine versifier. His **The Scribe Stood on the Village Street** reflects his difficulties in doing his job.

What ties many of these pieces together is their form -- a gentle parody of a well-known published poem. The last piece mentioned above is a parody of Casabianca ("The Boy Stood on the Burning Deck", 1826). **He Does Not Advertise** reflects Sir Walter Scott's The Lay of the Last Minstrel (1805) with its opening line "Breathes there a man with soul so dead…" Another such parody, **Kindly Mail Cheque,** encourages the errant subscriber through homely rhyme, and the structure is that of "The Old Oaken Bucket", a nostalgic tearjerker of 1817, widely known in North America, though almost a century old.

Ideally, the paper formed a connection with its readers, so that the paper reflected their wishes and needs. One piece is by such a reader, with a request that the paper start a "Poet's Corner". Wisely, the editor did not accede to this request, preferring to rely upon his own taste as to what his readers wanted. He published the poem (**Evening**) and accompanying letter, though.

Walt Mason, often called "Poet Laureate of American Democracy", was a prolific poet, whose verse was commonly not set in stanzas, but run on line to line, as if prose. His style was simple but workmanlike, and his poems were at one time published daily in more than two hundred newspapers in the United States and Canada. He was born in Canada but moved to the US at the age of 18. He spent much of his working life in newspapers and **The Country Editor**, which appeared in Princeton in 1917, is his reflection on the endless jobs of the editor.

Printing is not a clean job. As Mason says, one of his jobs was to "clean the grease from the printing press, with a bushel of cotton waste". The roller towel on the printing house door would also be used to clean things up, and **That Towel**, again widespread across North America, captures its foulness.

Newspapermen are both collaborators and rivals. One newspaperman writes a brief verse, which is published in his paper. Another paper picks it up and by "exchange" (a courtesy allowing other papers to freely reprint minor items), it is republished, but with an added verse; another paper adds yet another verse. Two examples, both from the *Coalmont Courier* and both from 1912, are **Caruso Poems**, dealing with the throat condition of that famous tenor, and **Mere Guesses**, having to do with the then-topical issue of suffragettes.

The competition between local papers often produced editorial comments and some verse, **Twinkle, Twinkle, Little Star** being one such, published by the *Courier* and directed at its Princeton rival. In it the writer refers to "pars", which are paragraphs, the unit of a stringer's work – longer than a sentence and shorter than an article. The Otter Ranchers mentioned come from nearby Otter Lake.

Ode (Owed) to the Gazoot is somewhat nastier in tone, reflecting the acrimonious relationship between the Hedley and Princeton papers. The *Hedley Gazette* was owned and edited by "Major" Ainslie McGraw, an Ontario man of Ulster heritage. He had been a newspaperman in Vernon and Midway in BC, and in Bruce County in Ontario. There is no evidence of him actually bearing a military rank. The moniker might have come from his combative nature and his jingoist support of the British Empire.

The hours of a newspaperman are long and tedious, and it must have been natural, as in many occupations, to cast oneself in an heroic mode. Our last piece in this section is **The Newspaper Guy**, a widely published and copied poem with many variants. It presents the newspaperman as he would like to see himself -- omniscient, omnipresent, and omnicompetent, even at the Golden Gates.

COALMONT

The Town of Opportunity

The rails have been laid into the town and Coalmont is now the new terminus, the base of operations for the next forty miles of railway building.

Before six months have passed there should be a payroll in Coalmont of between 350 and 400 men: This means population, which naturally means good business.

IF YOU ARE WISE YOU will invest in a little Coalmont real estate now while the choice is still good.

Don't let this opportnnity slip along with the others which have go t past you. Write for our circular and price list ; a post card will bring it to you. There are still some 50 foot lots left

Two blocks from the centre of town at only $225, $55 cash, bal. in 18 months to suit.

Williamson & Turner

AGENTS, COALMONT, B. C.

Soliloquy On The Procrastination Of Railroads

In the wild and woolly West,
Where we cannot get our paper,
Sure, we have to do our best
For the public here to cater:

So we borrowed from a friend
All his stock of 'wrapping brown',
'Cause the railroads wouldn't tend
To our squeals to bring it down.

It's been three weeks on the journey
Just from Calgary to here,
And the shipping bill says Kearney
Put it in with kegs of beer.
How we wish those kegs had rolled up
And our rolls of paper too,
Then we wouldn't need to hold up
Our subscribers as we do.

But the CPR is weary
And the GNR dead lame,
So our camps get good and beery
While they play this waiting game.
But we trust they will get moving
By a week more from to-day,
For the public aren't approving
Such ridiculous delay.

And it's apt to raise their dander
When they're always played for sucks,
E'en the solemn-visaged 'gander'
Now and then gets up and bucks
'Gainst this apathetic system,
Stalling freight goods for an age -
It makes us want to frisk 'em
And to biff 'em in our rage.

Oh! you CPR so weary
And you GNR dead lame,
Can you answer now this query:
Tell us where to lay the blame!

Coalmont Courier, 6 May 1912

He Does Not Advertise

Breathes there a man with soul so dead
Who never to himself has said:
"My trade of late is getting bad;
I'll try another ten-inch ad.!"

If there be, go mark him well,
For him no bank account shall swell;
No angels watch the golden stair,
To welcome home the millionaire.

The man who never asks for trade,
By local line, or ad. displayed,
Cares more for rest than worldly gain,
And patronage but gives him pain.

Tread lightly, friends; let no rude sound
Disturb his solitude profound,
Here let him lie in calm repose,
Unsought except by men he owes.

And when he dies, go plant him deep
That nothing may disturb his sleep,
Where no rude clamor may dispel
That quiet that he loved so well.

And that the world may know its loss,
Place on a stone a wreath of moss,
And on a stone above, "Here lies
A fossil, who did not advertise."

Similkameen Star, 12 June 1914

A Wise Geezer

There was an old geezer and he had a lot of sense;
And he started up a business on a dollar eighty-cents.
The dollar for stock and eighty for an ad.
Brought him three lovely dollars in a day, by dad!

Well, he bought more goods and a little more space
And he played that system with a smile on his face.
The customers flocked to his two-by-four
And he soon had to hustle for a regular store.

Up on the square where the people pass,
He gobbled up a corner that was all plate glass.
He fixed up the windows with the best that he had
And he told 'em all about it in a half page ad.

He soon had them coming and he never, never quit
And he wouldn't cut down on his ad one jit.
Well, he's kept things humping in the town ever since
And everybody calls him the Merchant Prince.

Some say it's luck, but that's all bunk -
Why, he was doing business when the times were punk.
People have to purchase and the geezer was wise -
For he knew the way to get 'em was to advertise.

Similkameen Star, 1 December 1916

Send It In

If you have a bit of news,
Send it in;
Or a joke that will amuse,
Send it in;
Or a story that is true,
An incident that's new,
We want to hear from you –
Send it in;
If it's only worth the while,
Never mind about the style,
We want to hear from you –
Send it in.

Princeton Star, 19 May 1922

The Editor's Plea!

We want News!
Ideas and views.
YOUR ideas and views of news.
News of parties, news of play,
News of what you do each day.
If your neighbour's dog has rabies
And mangled all the town's prize babies,
Please, oh! please, friend, don't refuse -
Phone it in, because it's NEWS!

We want News!
News to amuse.
Amusing stories all make news.
News that's sober, news that's sad.
ANY news will make us glad.
If you make a hole-in-one;
If you ever SEE it done -
Please, oh! please, friend, don't refuse,
Phone it in, 'cos WE WANT NEWS!

Similkameen Star, 27 February 1941

The Scribe Stood On The Village Street

The scribe stood on the village street
Whence all but he had fled.
There were no bosom friends to greet,
The place was nearly dead.

He started on his weary way
To rustle up some news,
But no one had a word to say;
They all were in the blues.

He got cigars and cigarettes
And Copenhagen snooze
And heard some sighs and sad regrets
But ne'er a jot of news.

And day by day, in every way,
There was less news to tell,
So said the scribe,
"If I'm a JAY, my job is surely 'ELL!"

Similkameen Star, 9 May 1923

Kindly Mail Cheque

How dear to our hearts is the steady subscriber
Who pays in advance at the birth of each year,
Who lays down the money and does it quite gladly,
And casts 'round the office a halo of cheer.
He never says, "Stop it; I cannot afford it,
I'm getting more papers now than I can read."
But always says, "Send it; our people all like it -
In fact we all think it a help and a need."
How welcome his cheque when it reaches our sanctum,
How it makes our pulse throb; how it makes our hearts dance.
We outwardly thank him; we inwardly bless him -
The steady subscriber who pays in advance.

Similkameen Star, 3 January 1913

Bert Thomas' horses coming through Princeton, 1943. The Allan Gill Collection

Twinkle Little Star: I hear that the Star, which has for some time past been interesting many people, has, owing to recent changes in the atmosphere, gained greater brilliancy and is becoming a familiar object in other places besides that in which it was first discovered. Those in authority have named it the Similkameen Star. Long may it shine! May I propose a "Poet's Corner" in the constellation and start it with the enclosed verses? I am, sir, yours faithfully, A STAR GAZER.

Evening

Twilight is come;
The day is gone;
The workers go home;
Their work is done.

Soft fall the shadows
Across the hills;
Night steals on apace,
For so God wills.

Sleep, weary toilers,
Shut fast your eyes;
Perhaps you may waken
In Paradise.

The moon smiles round
On the world asleep;
All is calm - not a sound
On the silence deep.

Similkameen Star, 25 October 1911

The Country Editor

"O come," I said to the Printer Man
Who edits the *Weekly Swish*,
"A rest will do you a lot of good -
So come to the creek and fish."

"If you'll wait awhile," said the Printer Man,
"I'll toddle along, I think;
But first I must write up some local dope
And open a can of ink,

"And carry in coal for the stove,
And mix up a lot of paste;
And clean the grease from the printing press,
With a bushel of cotton waste.

"And set up an ad. for the auctioneer,
And throw in a lot of type,
And hunt up the plumber and have him see
What's clogging the water pipes.

"And call on the doctor and have him soak
The swellings upon my head,
For I had it punched but an hour ago,
For something the paper said."

"I fear", I said to the Printer Man,
"If I wait till your chore list fails,
The minnows that frolic along the creek
Will be as large as whales."

Similkameen Star, 8 June 1917

That Towel

When I think of the towel, the old-fashioned towel,
That used to hang up by the printing-house door,
I think that nobody in these days of shoddy
Can hammer iron to wear as it wore.
The tramp, who abused it, the devil, who used it,
The comp. who got at it when these two were done,
The make-up and foreman, the editor, poor man –
Each rubbed some grime off, while they put a heap on.

In, over, and under, 'twas blacker than thunder,
'Twas harder than poverty, rougher than sin;
From the roller suspended, it never was bended,
And it flapped on the door like a banner of tin.
It grew thicker and rougher, harder and tougher,
And daily put on an inkier hue.
Till one windy morning, without any warning,
It fell on the floor and was broken in two.

Similkameen Star, 10 June 1908

Caruso Poems

Caruso's throat is normal,
His larynx is O.K.
His pharynx is in A1 shape,
His tonsils in full play;
His nasal passages are clear,
His vocal chords are sound.
Caruso's throat is normal -
Now let the world go round.

- *New York Tribune*

But how's his thyroid cartilage?
His glottis – does it work?
His epiglottis – does no germ
Within his weasand lurk?
His bronchia – can they project
A note with proper slam?
Is his esophagus all right?
And how's his diaphragm?

- *Chicago Tribune*

Don't you think that's personal?
How can we help but doubt
You're right to waybill poor Caruso
And turn him inside out?
So let his gullet go unmapped,
His diaphragm unwrung,
For what's the use if poor Caruso
Can sing the songs he sung?

- *Cleveland Plain Dealer*

Coalmont Courier, 20 May 1912

Mere Guesses

A suffragette
May fight and fight
And still look under
The bed at night.

- *Birmingham Age-Herald*

But if she found
A burglar there,
She'd yank him out
And pull his hair.

- *Youngstown Telegraph*

Or maybe she,
With courage grim,
Would pause to make
A speech to him.

- *Chicago Record-Herald*

All Coalmont Courier, 20 May 1912

Suffragettes in BC. P.J. Thomas Collection

Twinkle, Twinkle, Little Star

Twinkle, twinkle, little *Star*,
How I wonder who you are;
'Otter Ranchers' from afar,
Sending in their little 'par'.

Just to fill a tiny space,
Socking *Courier* in the face,
His must be a hardened case,
If he could but stand the pace.

'Ranchers' who talk 'boilerplate'
Surely must be off their pate,
And they'll only find their mate
In a print'ry up to date.

Coalmont Courier, 17 June 1912

Placer mining operation at Granite Creek. Princeton Museum

Ode (Owed) to the Gazoot

The following 'pome' was found on the road between Keremeos and Hedley. The author's name is unfortunately very indistinct owing to the action of rain and snow but looks something like this :
R...... d Kip......... ng

Oh, isn't it sad, I can't get an ad.
My poor dinky paper to fill,
It's really too bad, and driving me mad -
In fact I'm getting quite ill.

But the people all say that an ad. does not pay
When put in such a poor medium,
And that the twaddle I evolve from my noddle
Causes my readers great tedium.

But a soldier I am and I don't care a --(*word washed out*)
And a man that's not easy to baffle,
And my foes, I've heard say, ran away in dismay
When I drew my bright sword (*in a raffle*).

So don't think to destroy this bright soldier boy;
Many battles (*on paper*) I've seen,
But where bullets fly thick to my desk then I stick,
For my office is safer, I ween.

Let Kitchener prattle of bloodshed and battle;
The pen, not the sword, is the thing,
And with printer's ink black, I will lead the attack,
For that's how I fight for my king.

So, my Keremeos writer, you'll find I'm a fighter,
And a man that cannot take a hint,
And you'll find that I'm tireless, for I have tried wireless,
Road mending, and mining and print.

And I laugh at the man who fought in the Sudan -
I'm a much greater warrior, I think,
Though I've not faced a Boer, yet I have slain more
With my mighty pen, paper and ink.

So send in your ad. before I get mad.
If you don't, you are certain to rue it.
Though I never shed blood, yet I can scatter mud,
And you bet your sweet life, I will do it.

Similkameen Star, 20 February 1914

The Newspaper Guy

I see a man pushing his way through the lines
Of cops where the work of the 'fire fiend' shines.
"The chief?", I inquire - but a fireman replies:
"Oh, no! Why, that's one of those newspaper guys."

I see a man walk through the door of a show,
Where great crowds are blocked by the sign 'SRO':
"Is this man the star that no ticket he buys?"
" Star nothin'! He's one of these newspaper guys."

I see a man start on the trail of a crook,
And he scorns the police, but he brings him to book.
"Sherlock Holmes?", I inquire - some one cries:
"Sherlock H---! Naw, he's one of dese newspaper guys."

And some day I'll pass by the great Gates of Gold,
And see a man pass through unquestioned and bold.
"A saint ?", I'll ask and old Peter'll reply:
"No, he carries a pass – he's a newspaper guy."

Similkameen Star, 13 January 1909

Chapter 5: Sports

Sing a song of baseball,
Balls muffed on the fly,
Five and four Allenbyites
Knocked sky high.

When the game was opened,
Allenbyites thought it fun –
But wasn't that a mighty score:
What? Eighteen to one.

Modern life is hard to imagine without organized sports – no hockey or baseball games to attend, no teams to join, no games to be broadcast on radio and television, no sports section in the newspaper. We take sports for granted but it wasn't until the mid 1800s that organized sports began to take shape in Europe and North America. Team sports and codified rules of play originated in British "public" (that is, private) schools and began to spread across the western world only in the late 19th and early 20th centuries. Their emergence thus coincides with the settlement of western North America including the Similkameen valley. A number of factors contributed to this synchronicity.

Massive industrialization in Europe and eastern North America brought increased leisure time for citizens to participate in athletic activities and to attend and follow spectator sports. The widespread literacy brought about by the introduction of public education during the second half of the 19th century caused a surge in the publication of newspapers. Suddenly there were many more people who could read. Improved technology made large press runs easier, and newspapers more widespread and affordable. Newspaper stories about sports events caused an increase in sport's popularity as enthusiasts began following the exploits of professional athletes -- all the while enjoying the exercise and competition associated with amateur participation in sports.

Sports also tied in nicely with the boosterism of western North America; in fact, there was a strong connection between sports, boosterism, and nationalism. British public schools fostered team sports, nationalism and "manliness"-- it was from these schools, for example, that the first wave of volunteers for the First World War was drawn. The graduates of public schools were the leaders of British society and, with increased literacy and newspaper distribution, public school values soon spread to the population at large. The early settlers of the upper Similkameen were predominantly of British origin, and it was their sensibility that dominated what appeared in local newspapers. The *Similkameen Star* of 29 May 1912, in describing a Dominion Day baseball game, speaks of "the little breeze [that] unfurled the glorious flag that has led the world in civilizing and commercial influence..." Boosterism, with its tenets of self-help, positive thinking and conformity, were part of this sensibility, of which sports teams were an intrinsic part. The sports poems from Similkameen newspapers are suffused with the language of boosterism:

> We sometimes get beat but we only grin
> As the next time we play we try harder to win
> - Coalmont Ball Team

> And he is always chewing the fat
> But can't be heard for boosters...
> - Some Baseball Poetry

> Lacrosse is a game that makes manly men –
> A game which all men should play
> It has taken a hand in making this land
> The great nation it is today.
> - Lacrosse

This attitude to sports matches the desire to create a vibrant town that will attract settlers and investment. The existence of sports teams was one of the markers of a town's viability. This is still evident today, with reporters and fans in Canada talking about a city being "on the skids" when it loses its hockey team. In many ways the attitude towards team sports is another form of boosterism.

All the sports teams in the Similkameen were amateur ones and the keynote of the sports poetry in the local newspapers was "participation". In that respect, team sports, though they grew out of the public schools of the British upper class, were a social leveler and a source of social cohesion. If you played well, it didn't matter if you were the lowliest mucker in the mine or the mayor of the town -- your teammates and your town valued and embraced you. The playing fields also provided opportunities for townspeople to gather and catch up with the latest news, or to lay the groundwork for future business or organizational transactions. It was also a chance to socialize and compare notes with people from other communities.

At the turn of the century, baseball, which had evolved out of earlier British games such as rounders and cricket, was played throughout North America. The game was invented in the US and the rules were codified in the mid-1800s. In the Similkameen valley, baseball was a regular feature of Labour Day festivities. **Some Baseball Poetry** concerns games played between Hedley and Princeton in 1909, and in 1922 the poem **Coalmont Ball Team** names and celebrates the players on that team. It was composed by Jerry Brown, a local Coalmont character and the father of future mayor David Brown.

With the cold winters in the Similkameen, it is no surprise that ice hockey, a game first developed in Montreal in the 1870s, was popular in the valley. **Sing a Song of Hockey Sticks** celebrates the victory of the Hedley team over that of Keremeos in 1916.

Curling is thought to have been invented in medieval Scotland, now the home of the World Curling Federation. Many valley settlers claimed Scottish roots, and in 1929 the first curling rink was built in Princeton. There has been a curling club in town ever since. **Curlin' Weedy** ("weedy" being the Scots pronunciation of "widow") is the lament of a wife whose husband disappears from the home to curl until the ice melts in the spring. The narrator of **Declaration of Independence**, on the other hand, although having no particular affection for things Scottish ("My Southern ear is tortured by the wailing of the pipe"), is excited because he's "curlin' in the spiel!"

Lacrosse, like hockey, is also a Canadian game. It was originally played by eastern woodlands First nations, and picked up by settlers. It was eventually refined and codified in Montreal in the 1870s. The author of **Lacrosse** celebrates the joys of the game and its character-building quality. According to Laurie Currie, lacrosse was popular in Princeton in 1913, the year this poem was published.

Princeton's first ski club was founded in 1924. Land was cleared for a ski hill and a road and a cabin were built near where the Princeton Golf Course ninth hole is now located. The ski club participated in yearly meets around BC and the US. Granby Copper Company actually closed its mine during competitions so that workers could watch the races. The club was named the Amber Ski Club because when children broke their skis they were mended with tin from Amber Tobacco containers. In the 1940s, the Club even sent athletes to the winter Olympics. **Farewell to Skis** presents two opposing points of view regarding the end of the ski season.

Sports played a vital social role in the early days of the Similkameen valley. The emphasis on fair play and "doing your best" reflected the values of the predominantly British community leaders and fitted in nicely with the boosterism prevalent at the time. It also provided opportunities for isolated communities to come together and play, share news and socialize.

Some Baseball Poetry

After surviving the spring poetry season, the Gazette *has been stricken with an epidemic of baseball rhyme. The rival poets appear to have been plagiarizing from the same fount. If their play is as ragged as the poetry, it should be a snap for the other fellows. Better leave poetizing to the laureates and "play ball".*

First Dose

Roy is the pitcher,
Hill is at the bat,
John is the catcher
And you can't beat that.

They're all the finest players
And some time will champions be,
And carry away the pennant,
But that is 'twixt you and me.

Before their days are over,
Princeton they will play,
Out on the Reservation
On the 24th of May.

And you will hear their backers
Who think them very fine,
A-boasting just a little
Of the Hedley Baseball Nine.

Second Dose

Gus is the pitcher,
Hill is at the bat,
Bert is the catcher -
What do you know about that?

Captain Johnnie plays on first base -
Of course he is very good at that.
Roy is an expert on second -
What do you know about that?

Bob holds out on third
And he is always chewing the fat,
But can't be heard for boosters -
What do you know about that?

Billy plays in right field,
Harold in the left,
Edgar in the centre
Although he was too small to enter -
What do you know about that?

They are all the finest players
And sometime will champions be
And carry off the pennant
But that's 'twixt you and me -
And what do you know about that?

Before their days are over,
It's Princeton they will play
Out on the reservation
On the 24th of May -
And what do you know about that?

Hedley Gazette, 20 May 1909

Hedley Baseball Club July, 1938

Coalmont Ball Team

We come from the camp of mountain and snow,
Our rooters are known wherever they go,
For giving good sport which also is clean,
I'll bet we're the best that you've ever seen.
We sometimes get beat but we only grin,
As the next time we play we try harder to win,
And if we do win, you take it from me,
We're the happiest bunch you ever did see.

Our pitcher's name's Dick; his other name's Horne,
As genial a chap as ever was born:
When he pitches the ball to the man at the plate
He sure puts that batter in a terrible state;
He may make a swing to get a great hit,
But Dick threw a corker and the batter he bit;
He feels quite astonished as he hears a great shout;
Then he looks to the umpire, who bawls, "Batter out!".

Our first base is filled by a player so grand,
Whose parents baptized him as George McMahon.
When he's on to his game he's a hard one to match,
If the ball comes his way it's a dead certain catch,
And we've young Johnny Mac. who fills second base,
Who'd be a good player if he'd just keep his place,
And then we touch third, and I want to tell you,
You'll go a long way to beat Pettigrew.

We come now to Hogan who plays always short-stop,
And he as a ball player is right at the top.
To see him catch balls, then throw to a base,
Is a treat for to watch, as they land right in place.
Another player we've got who is brimful of pluck,
He goes by the peculiar cognomen of Chuck.
He keeps everybody cheery with his wonderful slang -
Why, you can't beat that fellow, just try what you can.

Then take our outfielders, you are always sure
That a half-decent ball won't pass Billy Muir,
And the fielder beside him, although he is tiny,
Is one of the best, though his nick-name is "Heinie",
He is easily the best we've got at the plate,
As the ball that he strikes goes at a terrible rate;
The outfielders may run and the ball they may chase,
But you can bet your sweet life that he's safe at third base.

And now comes our catcher, young Frankie McMahon,
You can't find his equal, just try what you can,
He's so smart on his feet and so sure to catch,
That it's really a pleasure his actions to watch.
Now this is the team that we have up here,
And although we have had a pretty good year
I just wish to add and you listen to me,
We'll even do better in nineteen two three.

Princeton Star, 13 October 1922

Sing a Song of Hockey Sticks

Sing a song of hockey sticks,
Puck shot everywhere,
Four and two Keremeosites
Right up in the air.

When the game was opened,
Keremeos thought they were it;
But wasn't that a mighty score,
Keep it dark – eight to nit.

Hedley Gazette, 27 January 1916

Curlin' Weedy

A' simmer lang, Ma Jock's been fine,
He's delved the yaird, an' cut the grass,
Built a new pailin' 'roon the lawn,
Pit new shelves i' the kitchen press,
Withoot a single word frae me.
He fixed a bing tae haud the coal,
He pit new shingles on the porch,
An' rigged me up a new claes pole . . .
There's no a thing A wanted dune
But he did for me richt away.
'Twas like Millaneum haud come;
That it waud lest, A could but pray.
An' whan the schule began again,
He'd tak' the bairns ilka nicht,
Heir Jimmie's readin', Phonnie's spells;
Seen Jeannie's sums were worked a' richt.
But noo - he gulps his sipper doon,
He's hardly time tae speak at a';
Wi' tam o' shanter on his heid,
He grabs his broom, an' he's awa.
Then till the sma' 'oors yont the morn,
Nae gliff o' him A ever sicht.
Till he comes fair rampagin' hame.
"Gosh! But the ice was grand the nicht!"
A see noo till the Spring does come
(For me it canna come ower speedie)
Oh! I'm nae longer Jock's guid wife.
A'm juist his "Curlin' Weedy."

Similkameen Star, 3 January 1949

Declaration of Independence

Oh, you can take the high road or you can have the low,
For north of Tweed or Solway I shall never care to go;
On the bonnie, bonnie banks of Clyde, you'll never see me roamin',
And I'll take your word for all the unspoilt beauty of Loch Lomon'.

I have no joy in Lauder, and Burns Night makes me tired,
By the excellence of Mountain Dew I've never been inspired;
What need for me to wander where the Grampians glower and gloom
When the heather of my England has a brighter, fairer bloom?

The Gaelic is all Greek to me, and when I write a pome,
Not even for the sake of rhyme will I say hame for home;
And where the Hielan' Laddie's gone I neither know nor care
(Beyond a bland suggestion that you might try Leicester Square).

The thistle's just a thistle, and a noxious weed, to me:
I've never heard the cows called home across the sands of Dee;
My Southern ear is tortured by the wailing of the pipe
And I'd pass the best of haggis for a mess of half-cooked tripe.

But when the frost is in the air and ice is true and keen,
When eight good sports are gathered and the game is close and clean,
And when my rock draws bravely in, and I am lying shot,
Why, I could praise the good Lord then, that He has made the Scot!

'Twas not to fill a column, nor to rile my Scottish friends,
That I have scrawled these stanzas; I have other, subtler ends.
Come closer and I'll whisper you the march I aim to steal -
Next week there'll be no Eston Press; I'm curlin' in the 'spiel!

Similkameen Star, 5 February 1942

Lacrosse

You may talk as you like about hockey,
While rugby's the sport for the fall;
But the game which is best, more speed than the rest,
Is the game of the 'crosse and the ball.
You may talk about football and cricket;
You may boast of your strokes and your drives;
But still just the same, it's lacrosse that's the game
When good old April arrives.

Then doff the shin pads and the sweater,
Hang your shillelagh up on the wall,
Take down the queer stick with nets and a crick,
Change the puck for the soft rubber ball;
And don your shorts and your jerseys,
Come out on the field with a run,
And handle your stick with a twirl and a trick
In the heat of the hot summer's sun.

Lacrosse is a game that makes manly men -
A game which all men should play.
It has taken a hand in making this land
The great nation it is today.
Then three times three for the game of lacrosse,
The manliest sport of all;
Hurrah to once more have a 'crosse in your hand
And to handle the small bounding ball!

Similkameen Star, 18 April 1913

Kettle Valley Railway tunnel. Similkameen River is in canyon to right of photo.
Princeton Museum

Farewell to Skis

The Pro's Farewell

When green has replaced this mantle of white,
And summer's return put the winter to flight,
What pleasant reminders of winter are these -
My toque and my mittens, my poles and my skis.

Farewell, my good friends, both worthy and true,
Farewell, 'til October again brings the snow,
And 'though for awhile the long winter flees,
My memories of you will remain, worthy skis.

The Novice's Farewell

With courage I climb up the snow-covered hills,
With patience accepted the curves with their spills.
While attempting to glide 'twixt the bushes and trees,
With what anguish received twisted ankles and knees.

How many's the morning I rose with the dawn,
(To please someone else) and put my skis on.
But now, for a spring and a summer and fall,
I can gaze with relief at my skis - on the wall.

Similkameen Star, 20 February 1941

Manning Park 1943. The Allan Gill Collection

Chapter 6: Mining

The history of the upper Similkameen, like so much of BC's southern interior, can be summed up in one word -- mining. Population growth and the establishment of towns were driven by the market for minerals.

The typical scenario begins with prospectors stamping the wild hills in all weathers. Opposing sentiments towards this kind of work are expressed in two poems. The narrator of **The Prospector's Ante-Mortem** thinks of himself as "a sort of king in a vast demesne". **The Mountain Grouse (or The Prospector's Lament)** on the other hand, complains about the snow and curses the poets who praise it. The opening of his poem is a parody of "Beautiful Snow" by American poet Joseph Warren Watson, whose poem begins, "Oh! The snow, the beautiful snow/Filling the sky and the earth below".

When a rich ore body is discovered, mining companies are formed and shares are offered. This process is lampooned in a song entitled **And He Never Came Back** that was sung in 1900 at a Christmas "Entertainment" in Princeton by a Mr. William Knight. The song was Knight's parody of a popular song of the same name composed by American songwriter William Jerome (1865-1932).

Investment in a prospective mine is followed by speculators advertising the birth of a new and soon-to-be-prosperous town. The mine opens and the town mushrooms into existence around it, complete with hotels, opera houses and saloons. A newspaper begins publication, sports teams and service clubs are formed and soon the town is "the biggest town west of Winnipeg". More often than not the ore is depleted or the price goes down, heralding the death of the town. Southern BC is riddled with ghost towns, most unknown and unremembered. Fire hydrants, old stoves and other detritus of abandoned towns can still be found in the woods of southern BC. Development in the upper Similkameen followed a slightly different trajectory. When John Fall Allison began ranching at the forks of the Similkameen and Tulameen Rivers in 1860, he heated his home with coal he had found on the riverbank. He supplemented his income by small-scale placer mining and later ran a trading post where gold dust was the medium of exchange. Allison noted the presence of copper, but with no roads and no capital, mining for coal or copper would have to wait. Low-level placer mining continued in the area until gold was discovered northwest of Princeton, setting off the 1885 gold rush in Granite Creek. By the turn of the 20th century, Granite Creek was already nearly a ghost town, but gold mining was beginning in Hedley, 40 kilometers east of Princeton, where it continued until 1955. In the 1960s, mining resumed there with the opening of an open pit mine, which closed in the 1980s. **The Old Pump** is written about the Mascot mine, one of the gold mines above Hedley. Water frequently seeped into mines and pumps were used to keep them dry.

It was necessary in Hedley, as in all such mines, to break down the large chunks of ore to a size small enough for processing, and the earliest way in which this was done was with the use of a stamp mill. Such a mill was built in Hedley in 1902. The stamps were large pestles with removable cast-iron shoes that crushed the ore. When a shoe broke, a tool called a hangup stick was used to immobilize the stamp so that the shoe could be replaced. **The Hangup Stick** describes the joys and pains of using this tool. The song is a parody of "The Old Oaken Bucket", a popular song composed in the 19th century that begins, "How dear to my heart are the scenes of my childhood…" Though the song was published in the *Similkameen Star* in 1900, the Hedley stamp mill was not completed until 1903. Whoever submitted it to the newspaper must have seen a stamp mill at work elsewhere.

Conditions in the early mines of BC were primitive, with much backbreaking work and few mechanical aids. The absence of electricity meant that the only light available was an open flame. The author of **A Miner's Candlestick** celebrates this small bit of light.

Coal seams underlie much of the Princeton area. Coal began to be mined in Blakeburn and Princeton before the First World War and continued in various locations until the early 1950s. In Blakeburn, teams of horses hauled coal from the mine high in the mountains down to Coalmont where it could be loaded onto rail cars. In 1920, these teams were replaced by an aerial tramway. Sections of this tramway still stand, surrounded by forest.

One of the bleakest days of coal mining in the area was what became know as "Black Wednesday". On Wednesday 13 August 1930, a huge explosion in the Blakeburn Number 4 mine in Coalmont killed all but one of the forty-six men working in the mine at the time. It was the fifth-worst mining disaster in British Columbia history. The community rallied around the bereaved families and a big fundraising campaign began. It is a tribute to the spirit and resilience of people in the area that a mere five months later, the rollicking **Blakeburn Song** appeared in the *Princeton Star.* The song was composed by Jimmy Colly, a Blakeburn miner.

In 1932, Tulameen Coal Mines Ltd. threatened the coal miners with a ten percent cut in pay. The miners responded by banding together and forming a union. A strike began in December 1932. In response, Princeton businessmen began a rabid anti-union campaign with inflammatory columns and editorials in the *Princeton Star.* They believed the strike was precipitated by Arthur "Slim" Evans who they branded a Bolshevik agitator. Groups of hoodlums with clubs and burning crosses tried to intimidate the mostly eastern European miners into abandoning the union. When fights broke out, Attorney General R.H. Pooley sent in the Provincial Police to assist in the suppression of the union. Evans was "kidnapped" by an unidentified "posse" and run out of town. The anti-communist hysteria in the papers is epitomized by the poem **In Memoriam** that claimed that the mines were closed and Princeton ruined because of "Evanskovich" (Evans) the "Red" and his cohorts. Eventually a deal was struck between the miners and the owners, but after the strike, many of the smaller mines in the area shut down. The depletion of the coal seams and the departure of able-bodied men for the Second World War spelled the end of coalmining in the area. Coalmont Collieries closed down in 1940 and by 1948 coalmining in the area had ceased altogether.

Copper claims were being worked on Copper Mountain, south of Princeton, as early as 1902, but because of transportation difficulties, no ore was shipped out until 1920. Granby Mining, Smelting & Power Col. Ltd. ran the Copper Mountain mine from 1925 until its closure at the beginning of the Depression in 1929. It was reopened in 1937 and ran until 1957. It reopened as an open pit mine in 1960 and closed again in 1996. The townsites of Allenby -- where the concentrator was located -- and Copper Mountain were laid out in the 1920s but have now disappeared with hardly a trace. With rising copper prices, the open pit mine on Copper Mountain has been refurbished and the Copper Mountain Mining Company reopened it in 2011.

The population of Princeton in 1901 was 316. By 1911, it had risen to 900. By the 1930s, it had climbed into the thousands and has maintained its present level of about 2500 to 3000 since the 1950s. Princeton has not suffered the fate of so many BC mining towns, for three main reasons: the diversity of mining meant that the town's economy was not dependent on the fickleness of the market for one type of mineral; cattle ranching has continued and grown since John Fall Allison first arrived; and the logging industry has been an economic mainstay for decades. These factors, plus the propensity of lower mainland folk to retire here, and the steady income from tourism, has saved Princeton from the ghost town fate of so many BC mining communities.

Horse-drawn ore cars at mine entrance, Copper Mountain, 1930s. Princeton Museum

The Prospector's Ante-Mortem

When I cash in and my game's all played,
With the last white chip stacked up and paid:
Don't shove me under the snug green turf
In the town where I am an office serf,
Don't put me down in a dinky plot
Where they bury 'em several to a lot.
No, ship me back to the hills I knew
Where I was a Man and a good man too,
A sort of king in a vast demesne,
Not simply a cog in a vast machine;
And plant me up on the mountainside
Where the cliffs are high and the view is wide
And the wind blows swift and keen and thin,
When I cash in.

When I cash in, though my ears will be
Quite deaf to the wind's shrill minstrelsy,
And the sounds I love I shall not hear,
I want to lie where the trail is near,
That the tread of the old prospector's feet
May shake the walls of my last retreat;
And the puncher humming a careless song
May stir them too as they ride along;
And even the thud of the miner's blast
May rock the ground where my bones are cast;
And I shall share in the miner's quest
And know their luck in my place of rest
Whether they lose the game or win -
When I cash in.

Coalmont Courier, 20 May 1912

The Mountain Grouse or The Prospector's Lament

Snow! Snow! Beautiful snow!
Where is the fellow who wrote,
"Snow! Snow! Beautiful snow"?
I'd like to get hold of the goat!
I'd bury him deep in his beautiful snow!
How would he like to be me,
Breaking a trail with a pack on my back
In snow well over the knee?
Six long miles to the railroad track
In snow to the top of the hill,
With a good round fifty pounds on my back
Up a grade that is fit to kill;
Snow on the ground and snow in the trees
That falls now and then on your head.
If you stop too long for a 'wind', you freeze,
So you plug to the top half-dead.

The idiot who wrote of the "beautiful snow"
Is the self-same silly moke,
Who talks at times with a poet's glow
Of the scent of the campfire smoke:
"Wreathing blue in the mountain air,
And curling up to the skies,
Dispelling thoughts of a town-bred,"
Did it ever get in his eyes?
As he dodged around a campfire trying to cook,
After a twenty-mile grind
'Cross wind-jams and rockslides? It does for a book,
But not for a prospector's mind!
I'd like him around when the skeeters are thick,
And you build up a darned good smudge,
I'd smoke him then till I made him sick
And he called his own poetry "fudge".

Similkameen Star, 9 February 1907

And He Never Came Back

A wily expert from the East,
To Copper Mountain went;
He said, "We've millions in New York,
For options I am bent."
He got one on a group of claims,
With lots of ore on sight;
And said, "I'll start a hundred men
When I return next month."

Chorus
He never came back, he never came back,
The prospector's head it is sore;
That expert he will kill, when they meet down in h---
Or up on that beautiful shore.

Similkameen Star, 29 December 1900

The Old Pump

The old pump works in the Mascot Mine,
Just off the track on the tunnel line;
And every time I pass its place
A smile grows right across my face,
For, no matter how hard its work may be
It always seems to say to me:
"It CAN be done, it CAN be done."

So I've often thought we miners, too,
Can learn from the pump a thing or two;
When the job is tough, the work real mean,
We lose a round with the bonus lean,
The shift, from the start, has been all wrong,
Just lend an ear to the pump's brave song:
"It CAN be done, it CAN be done."

Similkameen Star, 17 October 1940

Stamp mill interior

The Hang-Up Stick

How dear to my heart my remembrance of milling,
Reproduced are the scenes of my fancy so true;
The leaky ore-feeders that always were spilling
More rock on the floor than they ever fed through.

The wobbly old pulley, our camshaft adorning,
The menacing ore-bin that threatened to kill:
The two old cracked cams that were keyed every morning,
And the grease-reeking hang-up stick used in the mill.

That grease-garnished weapon I've grasped with a feeling
When often at noon from my luncheon I flew;
What a gift of profanity I was revealing
As I hung up a stamp that had broken a shoe!

The greasy old 'cam-post', the chain blocks hung near it,
The sledge and the drifts and the shims that don't fill;
And George's shrill whistle – a dead man could hear it –
As we rushed for the hang-up stick used in the mill.

But now far removed from that grease-smeared condition,
No tears of regret do my eyes ever fill;
Yet I hail as an old friend this pigmy edition
Of the grease-festooned hang-up stick used in the mill.

Similkameen Star, 23 June 1900

A Miner's Candlestick

Oh, my old candlestick, you're my constant friend,
Down under the ground where the shadows blend,
And a man's shut away from the good God's light,
From the blush of dawn to the hush of night;
Where a child's merry laugh, or a bird's low trill
Never can fall like a light, rippling rill
To sing to the miner of cheer in his home
And ring in his heart like an old love tome.
A drill makes the music that rings in his ears,
But a candle's the charmer to drive away fears.
Down deep underground where grim shadows are thick –
Here's to you always, my old candlestick!

Aye, many's the time we have had here at night
When darkness was playing tag with the light,
When the flecked clouds of quartz and the glint of gold
Spun themselves into dreams that cannot be told.
You're a weapon of war for the skulking foe -
My one friend that sticks, wherever I go.
Yes, grimy the hands are that swing the old pick,
But while there's yet life to our post we will stick.
The swing of the hammer, the ring of the drill,
Are dear to the soul of the miner still;
But mem'ries that stir me, and prove to be quick,
Are all twined about you, my old candlestick.

Similkameen Star, 14 July 1900

Men at Granite Creek, ca 1895. Princeton Museum

Blakeburn Song

Come all my friends and workers,
To hear me while I pray,
I've got a tale to tell you
About Blakeburn today.
It's a place high in the Rockies,
Ten thousand feet or more.
If you ever miss your step,
An awful fate's in store.

Chorus
When it's payday in the Rockies,
That's the time when it's gay,
For every one is full of life,
They turn life into day.
With a jolly glass to cheer them,
That's lots of fun, I'll say
Way high there in the Rockies
When it is pay day.

While sleeping in the bunkhouse
To pass the time away,
The super came to ask me
If I want to work today.
Then he says, "The mine is moving".
I says, "If that is true
Move it up to the bunkhouse -
I'll see what I can do."

Like soldiers in the trenches,
All's ready for a shunt,
For if the vendor's no beer
They make an awful grunt.
I am leaving work to others,
To all the married men,
In the Rockies it's payday -
I'm on the drunk again.

Princeton Star, 8 Jan 1931

In Memoriam
PRINCETON: Killed Winter 1932-33 by E. Evanskovich and his Dupes R.I.P.

Tread lightly, Pilgrim, on this sterile ground;
'Twas once a thriving, bustling town.
When the Reds came and took it o'er,
Prosperity went to a kindlier shore.
Evanskovich and his cohorts rule;
The "Red Flag" is now sung in school.
The mines are closed, the town is dead,
The children now cry out for bread.
So, Pilgrim, walk with muted tread;
You are passing o'er dishonoured dead.
Through cowardice, we must allow
That Evanskovich is ruling now.
AMEN

Princeton Star, 20 April 1933

Claude Snowden and George Shorthouse with an anti-union stunt, holding "Slim" Evans responsible for the "death" of Princeton, 1933. Princeton Museum

Chapter 7: To the Coast

"'A road! A road!' the people cry; to make our country rich and great!" So says a poem published in the 26 July 1900 *Similkameen Star* and such was the desire of the people of the upper Similkameen for nearly a century. From its earliest settlement in the mid-1800s until the completion of the Hope-Princeton Highway in 1949, the Similkameen saw itself as a neglected backwater. Its small population and geographical isolation ensured that it remained so for a long time; its cry for a transportation route to the coast went long unanswered.

Laying the Kettle Valley Railway track over Tulameen River near Princeton, 1915. Princeton Museum

The centres of population in early British Columbia were on the coast. The upper Similkameen is only 300 kilometers inland, but between it and the coast lie the precipitous Cascade Mountains. In pre-contact days, these were traversed occasionally by Similkameen First nations trading with the Stó:lo on the Fraser. The fur traders didn't travel this way until 1848, after the establishment of the Canadian-US border in 1846 forced the Hudson's Bay Company to use an all-British trade route to the coast. The furs travelled west over the Cascades on what later became a recreational hiking route known as **The Old Hope Trail**. Dave Taylor extols the beauties of this trail in his poem of the same name.

In 1860, gold was discovered in the Similkameen and in Rock Creek. The remoteness of these areas and their accessibility from the US prompted James Douglas, governor of the new Colony of British Columbia, to commission the Royal Engineers to survey a route, and contracted with Edgar Dewdney to build a trail from Fort Hope to Vermilion Forks (now Princeton). The road became known as the Dewdney Trail and follows much the same route as the current Hope-Princeton Highway.

Gold was discovered at Granite Creek northwest of Princeton in 1885. The upper Similkameen was also found to hold rich stores of platinum, copper and coal. However, the area's isolation prevented the effective exploitation of these resources. Without a railway there was practically no access to markets. From its inception in 1900, the *Star* spoke of the crying need for a railway to the coast.

The first railway builder to eye the area was James (Jim) J. Hill of the Great Northern Railroad (GN) in the northern US. He began construction of the Vancouver, Victoria and Eastern Railway (VV & E) north to Oroville, and thence across the border towards the rich mining areas of the upper Similkameen. This challenge to the hegemony of the Canadian Pacific Railway (CPR) caused it to respond with its own border-hugging subsidiary, the Kettle Valley Railway (KVR), to keep the Americans out of Canada. By 1900, the CPR had built a line west as far as Midway but financial roadblocks stalled further construction. The Similkameen people's ongoing frustration is expressed in the poems, "**The Prayer of the Similkameen Prospector**" and "**Wanted – A Railroad**" which castigate the CPR and the provincial government under Premier James Dunsmuir for their inaction.

The first line to make it into Princeton was the VV & E. It arrived in September of 1909 to a very warm reception – the Similkameen

River being unofficially renamed the "Jimhillkameen River" after the railroad's founder, Jim Hill -- but there was still no line to the coast. Frustration over this is expressed in the song "**Wait Till the Railroad's Finished**", clearly to be sung to the tune of "Wait Till the Sun Shines, Nellie". Finally in 1909, the VV & E and the KVR, anxious to avoid a continuation of their struggle, agreed that the KVR would share the VV & E's track to Brookmere, and access the CPR line down the Coquihalla River to Hope. The KVR reached Princeton from the east in April of 1915 but a connection to the coast had to wait until the Coquihalla Pass section was completed. Finally, in July of 1916, the line was complete and passengers and freight could travel from Princeton to the coast and back again.

Eventually, railway transport to the coast came to be taken for granted, and people in the Similkameen couldn't complain of their isolation. However they could complain, as Jay Ell did in **When We Get Up at Three in the Morning**, about train punctuality.

"Highway 3" near Hedley

With the advent of automobiles, the cry again went out for a road to the coast, reminiscent of that for a railway earlier in the century. Princeton sent several delegations to the provincial Good Roads League, and in 1923, the Vancouver Automobile Club, as a publicity stunt to draw attention to the need for a road, traveled with a pack train from Hope to Princeton over the "as yet unconquered Cascades". In the same year the *Star* published **Mister Gallagher and Mister Shean**, a parody of one of the most famous songs to come out of vaudeville, which asked, "When'll they build the Hope-Princeton Highway?" A year later "Jay Ell", the Star's Coalmont correspondent, in a poem entitled **A Pipe Dream**, asked a genie to intercede on construction of the road. Princeton's bid for a road to the coast was unsuccessful, however. Instead, in the mid 1920s, construction began in the Fraser Canyon for a road to the interior. After the flurry of articles in the *Princeton Star* during the early 1920s, very little was published in the newspapers about the Hope-Princeton Highway over the next decade.

During the Depression, thousands of unemployed single men travelled on the railways looking for work. In 1931, the BC government established "relief camps" for single men in isolated locations, putting them to work for fifty cents a day. The camps also served to remove the men from the public eye, and to make it difficult for them to initiate any political reaction to their situation. One of these camps was at Tashme – the current site of Sunshine Valley – and it was these men who worked on the Hope-Princeton Highway. At the same time, schemes were afoot to turn the Three Brothers area into a park. In 1930, Martin Grainger, a lumber businessman from the coast, who had been Chief Forester of BC from 1917 to 1920, wrote to BC's Minister of Lands Nels Loughheed with a plea for the establishment of a park. In the early 1960s, Dave Taylor, editor of the *Princeton Star* in 1931, wrote of a hiking trip he took to the Three Brothers area in July of 1931 with Bert Thomas, a local forest ranger and rancher, and Martin Grainger. Dave Taylor says that soon afterwards they "launched a province-wide campaign to bridge the twelve-mile gap of the Hope-Princeton Highway…on which work is now busily in progress. We had to support travel to the southern part of the province".

Five months after the July 1931 hiking trip, Taylor published the poem **The High Road** in the *Princeton Star* under the headline "Internationally Known Verses On Hope Road". The poem, written by the wife of the man in charge of construction, was likely intended as an encouragement to speed completion of the highway. Nowhere is it mentioned in the *Star* that men from the relief camp were building the road. When the relief camps, with their source of cheap labour, closed in 1935, work on the highway ceased.

The *Star* is silent about the road until 1937 when, with the road still not completed, it published a special edition on July 29 entitled "The Hope Trail Supplement" that outlined the commercial and recreational benefits of a road. It included maps of the old Hope Trail and of the proposed southern trans-provincial highway as well as Taylor's poem The Old Hope Trail. This supplement was a kind of follow-up to Taylor's and Grainger's attempts in 1931 to create a park and urge the completion of the highway. Manning Provincial Park was finally established in 1941. In the same year, still frustrated with the lack of progress on the highway, the *Star* published **Manning Park Reverie**, a poem which insisted that the "Hope-Princeton Highway must go through; Then tourists may your beauty view." A 1946 poem, **You Remember Too,** also praised the beauties of hiking the Old Hope Pass trail in Manning Park.

Manning Park, 1943. The Allan Gill collection

After a nine-year delay, construction work resumed on the Hope-Princeton Highway in 1944. Meanwhile, the only route to the coast was north from Princeton to Merritt, northwest to Spences Bridge, and thence down the Fraser Canyon. By early 1949 impatience regarding the road's slow pace of completion had reached the point that on February 17 of that year the *Similkameen Star* printed a "riddle" on the front page:

> The $64 question: which took the longest to build – the pyramids of Egypt or the Hope-Princeton road? (We can't answer yet – the pyramids are reported to have been completed)

In October of 1949, the Hope-Princeton Highway was finally opened and on 21 October the *Star's* headline reported: "New Hi'way Packs 'Em In Despite Snow". In spite of sixteen inches of sloppy snow, a total of 1600 cars arrived for the opening of the highway -- 200 had been expected.

Manning Park, 1943. The Allan Gill collection

The Old Hope Trail

Shoulder your packs, my hearties,
And let's be under sail,
For the world is waiting for us
Down the old Hope Trail.

The summer sun that's rising
Beyond the eastern rim
Too soon will scorch your shadow
As you jog abreast of him.

Though the Summit's miles be weary,
(And you may be sure of that),
We shall slumber 'neath the cedars
In the shade of Cedar Flat.

Far ahead the silvered Skagit
Where the rhododendrons grow,
And the rugged brow of Sawtooth,
With its coronet of snow.

A million colours dapple
The mantle of the hills,
A million sounds, a million scents,
And twenty million thrills.

A million rills that ripple
Rhymes too exquisite for men,
A million rocks to rumble
Their echoes back again.

A million flowers to tinkle
Like bells of silver light,
A million stars to twinkle
Through the canopy of night.

A sense of vastness grips you
When all is calm and still;
Man finds his true religion
In the silence of the hills.

And when the evening's heavy
With the drowsy drone of flies,
From out the glowing embers
The imps of fancy rise.

Among the cedar copses
Where deep Sumallo flits,
The shadow of the engineers
In mystic grandeur sits.

Then shoulder packs, my hearties,
And let good cheer prevail;
For the path of life is sweeter
Down the old Hope Trail.

Similkameen Star, 29 July 1937

1943 "reconnaissance" trip to newly-fomed Manning Park organized by the Vancouver Board of Trade and the BC Forest Service, Allan Gill collection

The Prayer of the Similkameen Prospector

From trails like Summit and Roche River camps,
Good Lord, deliver us!
From yellow-legged experts and his little 'knocker',
Good Lord, deliver us!
From incompetent road builders and their moccasin assistants,
Good Lord, deliver us!
From the Hope mountain survey fiasco,
Good Lord, deliver us !
From mossback engineers and 'has been' trail blazers,
Good Lord, deliver us!
From Dewdney, Carry, Dawson, Harvey, Moberley, et al,
Good Lord, deliver us!
From fool mining operators and 'windy' coal company promoters,
Good Lord, deliver us!
From an increase of the poll tax,
Good Lord, deliver us!
From the locking up of the Similkameen by the CPR,
Good Lord, deliver us!
From exploring feasible passes and wasting public funds,
Good Lord, deliver us!
And lastly, from a weak kneed government,
Controlled by corporative interests and run for
The benefit of those interests, as against the common people,
Good Lord, swiftly deliver us!

Similkameen Star, 17 August 1901

Nicomen Ridge, ca 1930. Princeton Museum

Wanted – A Railroad

The glinting waters flow between
High mountains, where Old Nature stored
In aeons past a precious hoard
Beside the winding Similkameen.

Bold seekers after treasure came
With daring hearts and ready hands.
(Obedient unto Hope's commands)
A share of Nature's wealth to claim.

By force they pierce the aged hills
And show their hidden riches forth –
While from the East, and West, and North,
The new-born land of promise fills.

"A road! A road!", the people cry:
"To make our country rich and great!"
"I fear you'll simply have to WAIT."
The Dunsmuir dummy-heads reply.

First Great Northern passenger train into Hedley, December 25, 1909

"The CPR is not prepared
To build the road at once, you see,
And WE don't like the VVE
For reasons we have NOT disclosed."

Poor Similkameen! Your crying need
Occasions but a passing thought:
'How easily public men are bought
As tools for corporation greed.'

The Star has much pleasure in publishing the above poem, which reached us by mail earlier this week. The author has not disclosed his or her identity, simply signing "Prospector," but we will be glad to receive any further productions, and wish to compliment our anonymous contributor on the style and sentiment of the verse – ED

Similkameen Star, 26 January 1901

Wait Till The Railroad's Finished

Wait till the railroad's finished
And the cars go rolling by,
We will be jolly fellows
Don't you sigh!
Down to the coast we'll wander,
Miss Popple and I,
Wait till the railroad's finished,
Bye and bye.

Similkameen Star, 3 June 1908

When We Get Up At Three In The Morning

When we get up at three in the morning,
Bemoaning our miserable fate,
And we head through the rain just in time for the train
To learn that it's four hours late.

Princeton Star, 5 May 1927

Finish the Hope Road

Shortest and Best Route to Interior

URGE COMPLETION OF THE PRINCETON, HOPE HIGHWAY

Trade Board Urges Finish Hope Road

Hope Road construction 1914. Princeton Museum

Mister Gallagher And Mister Shean

"Oh, Mister Gallagher! Oh, Mister Gallagher!
When'll they build Hope-Princeton highway, Mister Shean?"
"Well I can't exactly tell, when we're dead and gone to --
Maybe then they'll place a road upon the scene!"
"Why, Mister Shean! Why, Mister Shean!
On the day the cave-man carved the first tureen,
They were speaking of this road, and they will be when we've blowed!"
"Positively, Mister Gallagher!" "Absolutely, Mister Shean!"

"Oh, Mister Gallagher! Oh, Mister Gallagher!
Who's the girl that last night on your arm did lean?"
"Well I always hate to blow, but if still you want to know,
'Twas a Princeton Blue-bird was the girl you've seen!"
"Why, Mister Shean! Why, Mister Shean!
From most everything I've heard - or thought - or seen!
If a Princeton girl you mean, then she must have been a queen!"
"Positively, Mister Gallagher!" "Absolutely, Mister Shean!"

"Oh, Mister Gallagher! Oh, Mister Gallagher!
At the party last night you were - kinda keen!"
"Yes, I candidly admit that I threw a little fit,
When I kicked my heels and stood upon my bean!"
"Why, Mister Shean! Why, Mister Shean!
From most everything I've heard - or thought - or seen!
When you threw that natural fit, faith! You must have made a hit!"
"Positively, Mister Gallagher!" "Absolutely, Mister Shean!"

Princeton Star, 7 September 1923

A Pipe Dream

The Genie joshed with me one day
And said, "Cheer up old man,
If there is anything you wish,
I'll grant it if I can."

I said, "There's one thing I desire,
'Twould ease life's weary load -
If you would kindly have them build
The Hope to Princeton road."

"Before I grant your wish", she said,
"Please tell me who you are."
I said, "My dear, I thought you knew -
I'm on the *Princeton Star*."

The Genie vanished into space
But on my ear there fell
A far-off voice which seemed to say,
"O. G.! U. R. J. L."

Princeton Star, 4 January 1924

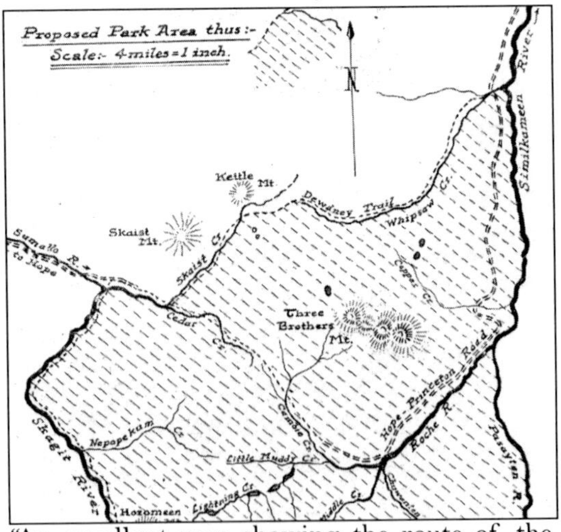

"An excellent map showing the route of the projected 'missing link' of the southern transprovincial highway and the proposed [Manning] park area. Construction has been carried forty-five miles out of Princeton. *Princeton Star* 11 July 1935

The High Road

Internationally Known Verses On Hope Road
The following poem, inspired by the Hope-Princeton road, appeared recently in the New York Times. *The authoress, Mrs. E.H. Clarke, whose husband is in charge of the construction work, is spending her Christmas at the road camp.*

Straight the slender pines trees stand,
Crowding to the sky,
Crowding close as if they know
Death is passing by.

Thunder blast and flash of steel,
Roar and dust and din –
So we build a new Highway
To let the people in.

Like busy ants, the great machines
Haul and load and haul;
Gouging out a mountainside,
Toiling at a wall.

Balanced on a shattered edge,
With scarce a foot to go;
Grinding forward, jerking back,
And the rapids sing below.

Tractors roaring in the mud,
Wheels that slip and spin –
So we build a new Highway
To let the people in.

Straight the slender pines trees stand,
Crowding to the sky;
Softly through the narrow aisles,
Peace is passing by.

Princeton Star, 24 December 1931

Manning Park Reverie

Up by the Falls Lookout,
Not far west of Copper Creek,
Manning Park lies round about
Calling all that pleasure seek.

Scenic beauty all year round,
Mountains, trees and echoes sound;
Trickling water, not far distant,
Down the mountain side resplendent.

Swings and benches here and there,
Carefree children playing near
Where deer by scores hop to and fro,
Unmolested fawn and doe.

Cars in throngs seek Manning Park,
Lovers stroll there after dark;
Hope-Princeton Highway must go through;
Then tourists may your beauty view.

Similkameen Star, 18 September 1941

Decal given out at the opening ceremony of the Hope Princeton Highway, 16 October 1949. Princeton Museum

You Remember Too

Thinking, as I sometimes do,
Of a journey once, with you,
Sixteen years ago, and plus -
Though it seems not so to us;
When, with pack and on Shanks Mare,
We climbed into alpine air:
Old Hope Pass! But at the crest
Puny pride shrunk in each breast -
Humbled at the magnitude
Of wild nature in the nude:
Other summits, vaster, steeper,
Towered above us; chasms deeper
Than the hollows we had crossed
Yawned below, with waters tossed
Into whiteness, into froth:
We were brothers to the moth!
And the glaciers in the blaze
Of soft sunshine formed a haze
And an iridescent air.
Then with pack, and on Shanks Mare,
On we plodded, westward ho;
Half a week, or more, to go:
Crossed the streams on shaky bridges,
Then along the Skagit ridges
To the rhododendron woods,
Blooming in the vast solitudes.
Camp-fire next, by the Sumallo,
Bodies tired, but souls of swallow:
One more day to go, and then
Storied Hope - and common men.
Pleasant retrospections all;
But since then, as you recall,
Sixteen years have gone to grief:
Time is such a sly old thief!

Similkameen Star, 8 August 1946

Perly Russell's Oldsmobile at Lover's Leap just east of Tulameen. Princeton Museum

Chapter 8: The Coming of the Car

Today those living in Princeton can visit friends in Hedley with just a 25-minute drive. Shopping for bulk organic produce requires only a 40-minute drive to Keremeos. Even Penticton, at just over 100 kilometers away, is not out of reach for Princetonites wanting an afternoon of shopping followed by supper in a restaurant. We take the radius of our social and economic lives for granted.

Things were different in 1900. A trip to Hedley took a day and Keremeos and Penticton required multi-day excursions. Commuting to a job that was not close at hand was out of the question. Towns were located right next to the mines that gave them birth, which is why so many of BC's early towns were located in isolated mountain valleys.

Before the arrival of the automobile, the upper Similkameen valley was a remote and lonely place to live. Even the arrival of the railway in the early part of the century did not eliminate the valley's isolation. Trains travel only at designated times and on designated routes so that, even after the railway arrived, many people in the valley still got around in wagons, on horseback or on foot. The continued predominance of horse travel even after the arrival of trains is evidenced by the continued appearance in the *Similkameen Star* of ads for livery stables. Laurie Currie in his book, *Princeton 120 Years*, says, "For one hundred years before the Hope-Princeton Highway was built, the horse had packed supplies in and out of [Princeton]."

In 1904, automobiles were common enough in British Columbia for them to be registered in Victoria; the Provincial Police issued license plates. In Princeton, however, the first automobile did not arrive until 1912. It was a Brockville Everett and was purchased in Penticton for $500 by W.H. Thomas. His son, Roy Thomas, said that the road from Penticton was very bad and that the car had so many flat tires along the way that his father swore he'd sell it for a dollar if he ever got to Princeton.

The first automobile-related ad in the *Similkameen Star* appeared that same year, in October 1912. From the Central Garage & Machine Company in Penticton, it advertised "Automobile Supplies". In the same edition, the Model Livery Stable offered the hauling of coal and the stabling of horses. Almost a year later, in August 1913, the Model Livery Stable added "& Autogarage" to its ad in the *Star*. This marriage of livery stable and garage continued until 1915, when ads for livery stables disappeared from the newspaper altogether. Stables did, however, continue to exist because Martin Grainger in *Riding the Skyline* speaks of using the services of a Princeton livery stable as late as 1929.

1913 marked a turning point in the production of automobiles in North America. That year, Henry Ford introduced assembly lines in his plants, which revolutionized transportation by revolutionizing industrial production. His manufacturing method became known as "Fordism", the mass production of inexpensive goods coupled with high wages for workers. Ford believed that consumerism was the key to peace. "Fordism" meant that automobiles, no longer novelty or luxury items, became affordable for large numbers of people. Compare, for example, the $500 W.H. Thomas paid for his car in 1912 with the $360 price for a Model T Ford in 1916. Model Ts became the car of choice and by 1918, half the automobiles in the United States were Model Ts. The car's popularity was due not only to its availability and low price but also to the fact that it was simply built and therefore easy to fix. Another asset was that it could negotiate the roughest roads -- a necessity in the Similkameen valley. These facts made the Model T a part of everyday life in the valley and gave rise to the first appearance of automobile poetry in the *Similkameen Star*.

Admiration for Henry Ford is expressed in **Henry Ford** -- sung to the tune of "Turkey in the Straw" -- that appeared in the *Star* in December 1915. **It's a Ford** -- sung to the tune of "Twinkle,

Twinkle Little Star" –- appeared the same year and sounds like it could have been an ad from the Ford Motor Company itself. Versions of both these songs were published in many places at the time and can still be found in the publications of antique car buffs.

In these days of rapid technological change, it is difficult to imagine the effect that the arrival of the internal combustion engine had on public sensibility. The horse -- which for thousands of years was used for tilling the soil, travel, and the transporting of goods -- had become obsolete. As a result, all the enterprises associated with the horse -- livery stables, the making of horseshoes, wagons, carriages, saddles, bridles and harnesses, the farms that produced feed, the freight companies, etc. -- also became obsolete and the people who worked in them were out of a job. Many of these jobs would have been local; they were replaced by anonymous assembly line jobs thousands of miles away. Martin Grainger, who wrote about the area in the early decades of the century, put it this way:

> The money that used to circulate in the district and make it prosperous when everyone rode or drove horses, and hay and grain were raised to feed them – this money drains away to the outside world in payment for second-hand cars and petrol.

The automobile also had a significant effect on social life in the upper Similkameen. In the early years of settlement, townsfolk made their own entertainment and towns were cohesive because travel was difficult. By 1915, the automobile was common enough that people began attending social events in other communities. The *Similkameen Star* in September of that year describes "several special automobile parties" travelling from Princeton to participate in Hedley's Labour Day dance. Automobiles also made extramural sports teams more feasible.

The early love affair with the automobile soon began to be tempered with an awareness of its destructive power. Even as early as 1904,the BC government passed the "Act to Regulate the Speed and

Operation of Motor Vehicles on Highways". Automobile accidents, often blamed on speeding, began to be reported in the newspaper. By 1919, the speed limit was 15 miles an hour in wooded country and 25 miles an hour in open country, although in the remote wilds of the Similkameen, the ability of police to regulate driving speed was probably limited and the condition of many of the roads in any event made speeding an impossibility. **The Joy Rider**, which appeared in the *Star* in 1917, was written by a police officer in Bellingham, WA, where roads were perhaps more amenable to speeding.

In the days before snowploughs, Similkameen winters would have seriously curtailed, if not eliminated, driving altogether. Spring was a chance to bring the Model T out of the garage or the barn and show it off. **The Frisky Fords** of May 1920 celebrates the dangers of out-of-practice drivers inflicting their vehicles onto the unsuspecting public on the muddy, potholed roads. The poem is by Tennyson J. Draft, an American poet of the first decades of the 20th century.

Ask the Man Who Owns One, which appeared in the *Star* in August 1920, continues with the theme of automobile safety but also alludes to the automobile as a status symbol. The title of the poem was the advertising slogan for the Packard, a luxury automobile produced by the Studebaker-Packard Corporation in Indiana. The poem ends with a note of envy towards car owners from one who owns no car – "You'd think I wouldn't have much fun/I don't". The poem is by the prolific Colorado poet, writer and journalist Claude Wiles Hallock.

By the 1920s, the automobile was here to stay and clichés about cars began to emerge. The now-familiar reference to women drivers and car salesmen described in **Teaching Them to Drive** -- a poem widely published in American newspapers of the time -- the used car cursed at in **The Second-Hand Car**, the amateur mechanic and the car that runs out of gas described in **The Village Motorsmith** became part of everyday culture. The poem, written by Doris Rail and published in several American newspapers, is based on Henry Wadsworth Longfellow's "The Village Blacksmith". **Such is Life**, published in 1931, introduces another car cliché, that of the traffic cop.

The degree to which automobiles and improved roads eroded the self-sufficiency of isolated towns in the upper Similkameen is demonstrated vividly by a St Patrick's Day dance held in Tulameen in 1929. On March 21 of that year, the *Princeton Star* reported that people came to the dance from the whole area -- Coalmont, Blakeburn, Princeton, Hedley, Keremeos, Merritt, the upper Otter Valley and Manning's Siding. Attendance from such a wide area would have been unthinkable in the era before the automobile.

Hedley baseball game ca. 1920

Henry Ford

There was an old man and he had a wooden leg,
He hadn't any money and he wouldn't beg.
He had a piece of pipe and a twelve-inch board,
Said to himself, "I'll make a Ford."

A gallon of gas and a quart of oil,
A piece of wire to make a coil,
Four big spools and an old tin can -
He hammered it together and the darn thing ran.

Hedley Gazette, 30 December 1915

It's a Ford

Beat it, beat it, little car,
How I wonder what you are,
Climbing up the hill so high,
Passing all the others by.

As it passed the first man fussed,
While the second mildly cussed,
But the last man yelled and roared,
"You can't stop it, it's a Ford!"

Similkameen Star, 22 October 1915

The Joy Rider

He always has the cut-out open, he always runs lykell,
He never stops for railroad crossings to listen for the bell.
He never gives you half the road, but like a hog sails by,
And lets you rustle for the ditch while he slams by on high.

He gets away with it awhile, luck simply hangs around,
Until the fatal day arrives and they pick him from the ground
And take him to the church yard near and plant him good and deep,
A warning to the damphools who the speed law never keep.

Similkameen Star, 4 May 1917

The Frisky Fords

Sweet spring has come. The little Fords
All from their holes crawl out,
And honk and rip and snort around
And gaily skip about.

They skitter here, they scuttle there,
And in their innocence
They knock down some old gentleman
Or climb up on a fence.

Ah, little Fords! When you were made
With so much skill and pains,
How sad that Henry couldn't find
A way to give you brains!

Princeton Star, 7 May 1920

Similkameen Star 21 May 1915

Ask the Man Who Owns One

Most motorists are blooming fools,
They trifle with the traffic rules.
I don't.

No man should try to get the drop
On any seasoned traffic cop,
Nor fail to heed his sign to stop.
I don't.

A man should never drive too fast,
Or brag about the cars he's passed;
I don't.

For Safety First should he his creed -
There really isn't any need
To drive a car at a feckless speed
I don't.

A man should never lose his bean
When piloting a gas machine.
I don't.

On city street or open road,
A man should never break the code,
Nor fellow-farers incommode.
I don't.

He should not scare equestrians
Nor chase the poor pedestrians.
I don't.

In fact, I have no car to run -
I'm shy the coin to purchase one.
You'd think I wouldn't have much fun -
I don't.

Princeton Star, 6 August 1920

Teaching Them to Drive

The Sweetheart

To learn to drive the auto, dear,
First push the lever into gear;
Then, push your left foot in like this;
That's fine! Now teacher gets a kiss.
Now, step upon the starter, so;
That makes the precious engine go.
Now let your left foot back like this;
Good! Teacher gets another kiss.
Upon the gas you must now step,
That fills the engine full of pep.
That's great! You are a clever miss.
Here, teacher gets another kiss.
Now change to second. Now to high.
You do that just as good as I.
Now stop the car right here, and then
We'll do the lesson once again.

The Wife

First, see your car is out of gear,
How? By this gear-shift lever here.
How can you tell? Why feel it, see?
The thing is simple as can be.
Now, step on that to make it start.
Great Scott! You'll tear it all apart
If you don't take your foot off quick
The second that it gives a kick.
Now throw your clutch. For goodness sake!
Your clutch! Your clutch! No, not your brake!
Why? 'Cause I tell you to, that's why,
There now, you needn't start to cry:
Now, pull this lever into low.
Step on the gas and start off slow.
Look out! You almost hit the fence.
Here, let me drive. You've got no sense.

Busy Salesman to New Driver

Here's your gas and here's your spark,
Turn your lights on after dark.
Here's your brake, emergency;
Here it's held in neutral, see?
Here it's low, and here it's high,
That's all. Don't hit a truck. Good-bye.

Princeton Star, 23 June 1927

The Second-Hand Car

"You low-down, no good, ornery bus;
I start you going, you fume and fuss,
Pant and choke and cough and wheeze,
You'd blow away in a good stiff breeze;
Your paint is dull, your tires are gone,
I curse you nights and at the dawn.
The glint is off your sides and hood,
I fear, old boy, you're done for good;
Full of knocks and twists and dents,
To me you look like thirty cents."

That's what the owner said as he
Looked down the street and saw poor me;
I'd trudged nine miles – that's much too far
In hunting for a good used car -
And then he praised that same old boat -
I must confess he got my goat;
He spoke in mellow, sweetened tones -
I bought that bus, eight hundred bones.

Princeton Star, 24 September 1920

The Village Motorsmith

Under a spreading chestnut tree
A stubborn auto stands;
The smith an angry man is he
With trouble on his hands.

The carburetor seems to be
The cause of all his woe;
He tightens half a dozen bolts,
But still it doesn't go.

He sits beside the road to give
His brain a chance to cool,
And ponders on his training at
The Correspondence school.

And then he starts his job once more
And just by chance 'tis seen
The cause of all his trouble is
He's out of gasoline.

Princeton Star, 6 October 1927

An early Princeton automobile

Such Is Life

We are hauled into court because we can't find work,
And our wives will testify that we are a shirk -
The judge says, "That doesn't sound so good."

Now we start for home in the old bus you bet -
We are just about as hungry as we can get.
So we speed up a little to get home quick,
And we get soaked ten bucks for speeding.
Wouldn't that make you sick?

Now we get a little down in the dumps,
And we drink a little something to help us over the bumps.
The old black Maria hauls us down the line,
The darned old judge hands a ten-dollar fine.

We get disgusted with married life,
And run away from a bunch of kids and a wife.
We are hauled into court and the judge with a smile,
Gives us ninety days on the old rock pile.

We take our girl for an auto ride
And we put one arm around her close by our side.
But the traffic cop grabs us for driving with one hand
And the judge gives us ten days in the old can.

Princeton Star, 1 October 1931

Chapter 9: The Valley and the War

The First World War, the end of a century of near peace, and the beginning of the most violent century ever, left 37 million dead. The Similkameen valley contributed its share to this cataclysm. Some scores of men left the valley over the course of the First World War and many never returned. Princeton can account for 16, Hedley 11 and Keremeos 10 dead. Those soldiers from the smaller communities of Allenby, Coalmont, Tulameen, Ollala, and Cawston are commemorated, if at all, on one of the war memorials in the larger towns. Princeton built theirs in the early 1920s.

Why did they go so far, and in what cause? The assassination of an Austrian Arch-Duke may have been the trigger, but it could never have been the cause. The cause was the intricate links of obligations that bound nation to nation. Austria wanted to punish Serbia for the assassination, Russia wanted to defend Serbia, Germany wanted to defend Austria, France was linked by treaty to assist Russia, Britain was linked by treaty to defend France. Thus the First World War – but what linked Canada to Britain?

The poems published in the valley's presses tell us. The colonies were Britain's children, and it was their duty to defend the mother country. These poems are drawn in the main from Britain, but one, **Our Duty**, saw publication first in the *Montreal Evening News* and may have been made here, and another, **The Union Jack**, though anonymous, appears in pre-War Canadian books and papers.

Wars need heroes and villains. The Allied hero in song and poetry was the British Secretary of State for War, Lord Kitchener, whose death at sea in 1916 was mourned in song and poetry. **Kitchener**, by Manitoba's Robert J.C. Stead, is typical of the genre. The villain, for there was only one, was the Kaiser. An early poem excoriating him appeared in the Hedley paper four years before the start of the war, and was made in Montreal by A. McGregor Rose, writing under the name of A.M.R. Gordon. His **Hoch der Kaiser** of 1897 was the cause of a scandal when it was recited by a US Rear Admiral at a banquet in 1899. Both Hedley and Princeton papers republished it, and both also printed a parody of it, which included mention of President Teddy Roosevelt. The song **It's a Long, Long Run to St. Helena**, a fine parody of the all-time favourite of English-speaking soldiers, "Tipperary", compares the Kaiser with Napoleon, and foresees the same exile for him.

More typical and perhaps more representative are the poems written from the stance of the ordinary people. **Songs of a Simple Tommy** was made by a private from Merritt, and **Mother o' Mine** was written in 1916 by a soldier's mother from Boissevain,

First World War recruitment poster. P.J. Thomas Collection

Manitoba. Both present the view from the trenches, and both mention the joy of incoming mail (rather than incoming shells). More mordant is **Wartime Mother Goose Parodies**, with its bitter reflections on hardship and injustice at home.

The tragedy of the Great War, as it was soon called, is brought down in **Fisherman's Rest** to the loss of a friend and the natural world he loved -- the coyote, the deer, the loon, the trout, even the bush-tail rats who have taken over his now empty cabin. But saddest of all is the little four-liner titled **War and Cider**, printed just eighty days after Canada entered the War, when it could still be imagined that the boys would be home by Christmas.

Our Duty

I'm a native son of Canada – a clerk by occupation,
I know it is a humble one, but helps to make a nation;
I'm of peaceful disposition, but I'll never shirk a fight
If I think my help is needed and I know the cause is right.

Now old John Bull's in trouble, and is loading up his guns,
And I know, though he's not asked it, that he counts upon his sons;
So it's up to us Canadians to give all the help we can.
I don't know if all are ready, but you bet your life I am.

Of course I'm not a regular, and have not been trained like some,
But when a man is willing I'm sure that can be overcome.
I do not seek adventure or a trip across the sea,
I just feel it my duty - and that's good enough for me.

For John Bull gives us freedom, treats us like a grown child,
Though sometimes we've been thoughtless and inclined to running wild.
But now that he's in trouble, and needs all his family's aid,
Canada, his oldest son, should see their debt is paid.

Hedley Gazette, 29 October 1914

The Union Jack

It's only a small bit of hunting,
It's only an old coloured rag,
Yet thousands have died for its honour,
And shed their best blood for the flag.

It's charged with the cross of St. Andrew,
Which of old Scotland's heroes has led;
It carries the cross of St. Patrick,
For which Ireland's bravest have bled.

Joined with these on our own English ensign
St. George's red cross on white field,
Round which from King Richard to Wolseley,
Britons conquer, or die, but ne'er yield.

It flutters in triumph o'er ocean,
As free as the wind and the wave;
And bondsmen from shackles unloosened,
'Neath its shadows no longer a slave.

It floats over Cyprus and Malta,
O'er Canada, the Indies, Hong Kong;
And Britons where'er their flag's flying,
Claim the right which to Britons belong.

We hoist it to show our devotion
To our Queen, to our Country, our Laws;
It's the outward and visible emblem
Of advancement and liberty's cause.

You may say it's a small bit of bunting,
You may call it an old coloured rag:
Yet freedom has made it majestic
And time has ennobled the flag.

Hedley Gazette, 15 October 1914

Kitchener

Weep, waves of England! Nobler clay
Was ne'er to nobler grave consigned.
The wild waves weep with us today
Who mourn a nation's master-mind.

We hoped an honoured age for him
And ashes laid with England's great;
And rapturous music; and the dim
Deep hush that veils our Tomb of State.

But this is better. Let him sleep
Where sleep the men who made us free;
For England's heart is in the deep,
And England's glory is the sea.

One only vow above his bier,
One only oath beside his bed;
We swear our flag shall shield him here
Until the sea gives up its dead!

Leap, waves of England! Boastful be,
And fling defiance in the blast,
For earth is envious of the Sea
Which shelters England's dead at last.

Hedley Gazette, 31 August 1916

Hoch Der Kaiser

Der kaiser auf der vaterland
Und Gott on high all things gommand.
Ve two! Ach! Don'd you understahnd?
Meinself - und Gott!

Vile some men sing the bower divine,
Mein soldiers sing "Die Wacht am Rhine."
Und drink der healt' in Rhenish wein,
Auf me - und Gott!

Dere's France dot swaggers all aroundt:
She's ausgespieldt! She's no aggroundt
To much, ve dinks, she clon'd amoundt;
Meinself - und Gott.

She vill not dare to fight again;
But if she should I'll show her blain
Dot Elsass und (in French) Lorraine
Are mein, by Gott!

Dere's gran'ma dinks she's nicht shmall bier;
Mit Boers and dings she interfere.
She'll learn none owns dis hemisphere
But me - und Gott!

She dinks, goot frau, some ships she's got
Und soldiers midt der scarlet coat -
Ach ! We could knock dem – pouf - like dot!
Meinself - und Gott!

In dimes auf peace brepare for wars,
I bear der helm und spear of Mars
Und care nicht for ten thousand czars -
Meinself - und Gott !

In short, I humor every whim,
Mit aspect dark und visage grim.
Gott pulls mit me und I mit him -
Meinself - und Gott!

Hedley Gazette, 20 August 1914

It's A Long, Long Run To St. Helena

Billy had a notion he could make the nations dance;
First he'd slaughter Belgium, then he'd tackle sunny France;
England was so little, and her army was so small,
He'd simply o'er the channel cross and watch the kingdom fall.

Chorus
It's a long run to St. Helena, it's a long run by sea;
It's a long run to St. Helena, to the place prepared for me.
Good-bye scraps of paper, farewell Europe fair,
It's a long run to St. Helena, but I'll soon be there.

Russia may be mighty and her Cossacks may be tall;
Billy was undaunted, he could eas'ly lick them all.
Paris, Calais, Dover in their turn would bite the ground,
While over in Old England he would surely then be crowned.

It was little Belgium put the kink in Billy's pride;
France and England held the day while Russia got her stride.
Billy got excited when he couldn't reach the sea,
And shouted, "It's the world that's bad, don't lay the blame on me."

Hedley Gazette, 4 March 1915

Hedley soldiers heading home from the First World War

Songs of a Simple Tommy

MERRITT SOLDIER WRITES GOOD VERSE FOR PASTIME

Hugh Campbell of this city has received the following verses from his son, Pte. Dave Campbell, who is now serving with the Canadian army "Somewhere in France". The many friends of this jolly young soldier will recognize at once that the author could be none other than he, for the expressions are peculiarly Davie's.

If your sleeping place is damp, never mind;
If you wake up with the cramps, never mind;
If your tent should tumble in and relieve your nose of skin,
While the Sergeant drinks your gin, never mind.

If you have to rise at four, never mind;
If the morning's dark and raw, never mind;
If your matches should elope with your only piece of soap
And you have to bum and grope, never mind.

If your inch of pork should freeze, or you find
A snail upon your cheese, never mind;
If a 'coal box' should make hay of the old YMCA
And your coffee melts away, never mind.

If the cook's a trifle new, never mind;
If you get your tea and stew, never mind;
And you find your pint of pice has a muddy coat of ice,
Try to think it's jolly nice - never mind.

Keep a steady upper lip and you'll find
Every cloud you like to rise silver-lined;
Though the skies are looking grey, yet it's ten to one there may
Be a parcel on its way, so never mind.

Similkameen Star, 1 February 1918

Mother o' Mine

Mother o' mine, you will never know
What mail time means to us,
Out in the front line trenches,
In all that awful fuss.

With Fritz's high explosives
Dropping round like hail,
And our pals, God help them! in pieces,
We watch for the overseas mail.

When we sit in a rotten dugout,
With the roof just caving in,
Feeling not what you would call happy
With the sights that we have seen

The mail comes in - believe me,
We're glad that we're alive:
And the seas between us are like a dream
The day the mail arrives.

We forget the awful horrors
When we touch what you have knit.
And the mud and water up to our knees,
Don't bother us a bit.

And the eats! Say, they are scrumptious,
We are sorry for the boys
Who petered out before they came -
We'd like to share our joys.

I'm back in the trenches tomorrow,
After a three days' spell
At rest camp, I'm not dead anxious
To be back again in that hell.

But it helps a lot when at mail time
We find we're not forgot,
By the ones at home, now, so long, dear,
(That's a tear, please excuse the blot.)

Similkameen Star, 5 April 1918

Wartime Mother Goose Parodies

Jack Spratt could eat no fat,
His wife could eat no lean,
Until they hocked the family plate
And sold the limousine.

Peter, Peter, pumpkin eater,
Had a wife and couldn't keep her;
On the streets he had to beg
Because she craved a daily egg.

Tom, Tom the piper's son,
Stole a pig and away he run.
He stole the pig at the County Fair -
And now he's a multimillionaire.

Similkameen Star, 12 October 1917

Fisherman's Rest

The bush-tails hold revel today,
'Mid the dust fast mouldering there,
The coyotes pass on their way,
To hunt the deer from his lair.

He called it the Fisherman's -
A real good rest you could take,
If you listened to Jack's behest
To go to his home on the Lake.

And many's the hour I have spent,
As we fished for trout with a trawl,
And my heart was full of content,
When Jack caught the biggest of all.

Then the fish would rise to a fly,
Or we'd pull ashore for a spell,
Or list to the loon's plaintive cry,
Which the echo re-echoed so well.

And Jack was so gentle and good -
He'd ever some homeless one there.
The shack at the edge of the wood
Had always a bed still to spare.

The bush-tails hold revel today
'Mid the dust fast mouldering there,
The coyotes pass on their way,
To hunt the deer from his lair.

And the snow drifts high on the door,
Where the fire is now quenched for aye,
For the Rest-maker comes no more.
He has gone to rest in the sky.

In France his body lies sleeping,
His soul was that Fisherman's true,
Who Jack now surely is keeping,
To rest with a Fisherman too.

Similkameen Star, December 1917

War and Cider

Then sweet November will return
With Winter's scouts beside her,
And we shall turn from war's concern
To fixing apple cider.

Similkameen Star, 23 October 1914

Chapter 10: Prohibition

The word "prohibition" is associated in many Canadians' minds with the United States, with Al Capone, and the beginnings of organized crime. Few Canadians remember a time when Canada was dry, too.

Prohibition, a ban on the manufacture and sale of alcoholic liquor, was brought about by a growing international movement at the end of the 19th century. The industrial slums in Europe and North America, were "ground zero" for suffering, poverty, diseases and early deaths, and these conditions were thought to encourage many a working man to drink to forget his troubles. "The pub door", they said, "is the quickest way out of Salford," one of the more notorious slums of the Manchester area. Drinking and drunkenness only made such life situations worse.

The temperance movement, as it was called, drew strong support from Presbyterians and Baptists and from other groups who advocated for "total abstinence" as a path to social progress. The campaign for prohibition paralleled another campaign, that for "votes for women". They had a common element: women, in their ultimate roles as mothers of the family and of the nation, were commonly thought of as being purer and more decent than men, and when they had won the vote, they would use it to make a purer and more decent society. These groups – The Sons of Temperance, the Royal Templars of Temperance, the Independent Order of Good Templars, and the Women's Christian Temperance Union (WCTU), used meetings, posters, and songs to get their message across, and one can still come across such songbooks in second hand bookshops. Phil Thomas collected this example in Heffley Creek in 1964:

> I will paint you a signboard, rumseller,
> And hang it above your door,
> A better and truer signboard
> Than ever you've seen before.

I will paint with the skill of a master
And many will stop to see
This wonderful piece of painting,
So like the reality.

It ends with:

And here is the form of the mother
As she kneels by her darling's side -
Her beautiful boy that was dearer
Than all in this world beside.
And here is the form of the coffin,
Labelled with one word 'Lost' -
I will paint you all this, rumseller,
I will paint it free of cost.

The temperance movement in Canada was strong enough in 1898 to bring about a referendum, in which, of course, only men were allowed to vote. Every province except Quebec voted in favour, from a high of 89.2% in Prince Edward Island to a low of 54.6% in BC. Quebec's vote was the mirror image – 81.2% opposed the idea. Liberal Prime Minister Laurier thought that the national vote, divided down the middle as it was - 51% to 49% - and the second largest province unalterably opposed, were good reasons not to proceed with temperance as a policy.

The beginning of the First World War in 1914 exacerbated the perceived problem of alcohol consumption. People were expected to make sacrifices -- King George V himself urged that grain should be used for food, not liquor.

In BC, many could see the inevitable. "The following sad sight," reported the *Similkameen Star* 12 May 1916, "as depicted by the *Mohave Miner* will soon pass away in many parts of America, for soon the beer will ride upon its bier, to lands where schooners are unknown, and the growler never comes". Here is what *The Miner* says:

Alone on the depot platform,
Bathed in the cold winter breeze,
Stands an empty eight-gallon beer keg
With nothing in it to freeze.

Shorn of its lost former glory,
Drained of its last amber dreg –
Beerless, bungless and friendless –
Stands an empty eight-gallon keg.

The temperance forces in BC were aligned with the Liberal Party, and opposed the sitting Conservative premier W.J. Bowser, a man well known for his connections with railway developers, land speculators and liquor interests. When the provincial election was called for September 1916, these progressive forces managed to have two referenda added to the vote: the first, whether there should be prohibition of the sale of alcoholic beverages in BC, and the second, whether the right to vote should be extended to women. The government was soundly defeated, and both referenda passed. The votes for women referendum won handily, but the other win was much more marginal – 54% to 46%. Princeton was close to the provincial average at 52.9%. These figures did not augur well for the success of the coming legislation.

BC went officially "dry" on 1 October 1917, and stayed dry until 15 June 1921. Like every other "dry" place, drinkers found, or thought they found, solutions. For example, liquor was allowed "for medicinal purposes", which required, of course, a prescription. "Foiled", outlines the attempt for one:

"I think I have the flu," he cried,
In tones of deep despair.
"No booze," the stern old Doc replied
With most unmoistful air.
And so the painful patient sighed
And went away from there.

Similkameen Star, 13 August 1920

But help was on the way for the "wets". At the next election, held 20 October 1920, another referendum was added, asking whether prohibition should continue, or whether there should be government control on the distribution of liquor. The electorate decided overwhelmingly for the latter. The Similkameen valley communities voted 63% to 37%.

Following the referendum, new legislation allowing the purchase of "spirituous and malt liquors" in "sealed packages", and resulted in the introduction of government liquor stores in June 1921. The following appeared 20 October 1922 in response, by "Jay Ell", the *Star's* Coalmont reporter:

Since the Government Liquor Store Opened

"When we got dry – in days of yore,
We patronized the Princeton store;
But, "quoth the tailor, "Never more;
Them days are gone forever."

Similkameen Star, 20 October 1922

Phil Thomas collected a song in Princeton in October 1963 on the same subject:

Come all you coal miners from the old Tulameen,
You drunkards and boozers that you might have been.
You may have a dollar, you may have had more,
But you spent it on booze at the old liquor store.

When you are old and too aged or blind
To make your own living down in the coal mine,
They'll send you a pension till life's journey's o'er
On the profits they made at the old liquor store.

A government liquor store was still not enough for the liquor interests, who sought to get back the business of selling liquor from the government. A "Moderation League" appeared, running ads in local papers and urging "beer by the glass". They wanted the Liquor Control Commission to have the power to authorize the sale of beer by the glass, during limited hours, in approved establishments where meals were served, and the discretionary power to cancel this privilege. Beer was not to be sold in a bar. Yet another referendum was planned, this time in conjunction with the next election, in June 1924. The campaign succeeded, and the familiar "beer parlors" appeared in "licenced premises", mostly local hotels. The Princeton vote was 293 in favour of this moderated approach, and 48 against it.

The killjoys had their way, nonetheless. The following 1925 regulation under the Government Liquor Act decreed the end of song and music in pubs, much as Lloyd George's similar bill did in the UK:

> No licensee shall permit any person to play any game or sport or to dance upon his licensed premises. No licensee shall keep ...any musical instrument ...(or)...permit any person to play any musical instrument ...(or)...under any pretext or device whatsoever, furnish or cause to be furnished any music in the sales-room of the licensed premises.

That drinking should be associated with pleasure was no longer a notion to be countenanced, in spite of the sentiments of our last piece:

Why Man Lives A Long Life

The horse and mule live thirty years,
And nothing know of wines and beers;
The goats and sheep at twenty die,
And never taste of Scotch and rye;
The cow drinks water by the ton,
And at eighteen, is nearly done;
The dog at fifteen cashes in,
Without the aid of rum and gin;

The cat in milk and water soaks,
And then in twelve short years he croaks;
The modest, sober, bone-dry hen
Lays eggs for 'nogs and dies at ten;
All animals are strictly dry,
They sinless live and swiftly die;
But sinful, ginful, rum soaked men,
Survive for three score years and ten,
And some of us, the mighty few,
Stay plastered till we're eighty-two.

Similkameen Star, 21 January 1943

P.J. Thomas Collection

Chapter 11: Making Ends Meet

It's often hard to remember, but until the 1950s, most people had to struggle to "make ends meet", a phrase that itself goes back to at least the 1650s. The twentieth century was not kind to people born shortly before its beginning: youth taken up with the First World War, most of mature life struggling with the Depression, followed by the Second World War; and some degree of relative comfort only in retirement.

The songs and verses made for common consumption reflected this anxiety about getting enough to eat and to live on, sometimes in sadness but more often with a wry and caustic realism. Our first verse, **Why They Don't Enlist**, is an American parody of one of Rudyard Kipling's most successful poems, "Danny Deever", made in 1890. Kipling's poem is a conversation between a sergeant and a private at the scene of an execution of Deever, who "shot a comrade sleepin'" and must therefore hang. The parody follows the structure of the original but replaces what had been a conversation of horror by one of humour. It appeared in the *St. Louis Post Dispatch* and was reprinted in the *Hedley Gazette* in 1908.

Recessions have been with us for a long time, and they turn up with regularity. The first recession of the 20th century occurred between 1910 and 1912, and brought forth three verses, all appearing in the *Coalmont Courier* in 1912. **Try This on Your Clavier** is again a parody, this time of "The Flowers That Bloom in the Spring" from Gilbert and Sullivan's "Mikado" of 1885. The next of the Coalmont verses, **The Average Income**, doesn't seem to have come from a mining family; the stanza about the cook and the "serving maid" and the crack about strikes suggest someone much better off than the average Coalmonter. We are reminded of the poem written by a schoolgirl from a wealthy family, asked to write about "A Poor Family". "There was once a family," she wrote, "that was very poor. The father and mother were poor, the children were poor, the cook and the gardener were poor, the maid and the chauffeur were poor…." The last of these three 1912 Coalmont verses, **The Ultimate Victim**, was drawn from the pages of the *Chicago Post*; it's a complaint by a storekeeper about being blamed for high prices. He seeks to blame others in the chain of production from farm to store, notably the broker, the railroad, and the middleman. The second verse we have added from a set found in the Wellington, New Zealand *Evening Post* in August 1935. The structure suggests that it was a song – possibly "D'ye Ken John Peel?" a song every schoolchild in Canada was taught in the interwar period.

The economic uncertainty that followed the First World War and intensified during the Depression produced its own verses. **Heaven's Enough for Him** tells the story of a grocer who "worked hard night and day" but never got rich because of the many patrons who didn't pay their bills. But instead of asking why they couldn't pay their bills, the grocer, lacking any sense of class consciousness, "wished for nothing more" than to "watch them sizzle and burn" in hell.

The same tone is taken in **The Farmer**, published at the beginning of the 1930s. Here the farmer, rather than the grocer, states that *he's* not to blame. The verse may be a response to "The Farmer is the Man", drawn from the Populist movement of the 1890's, a widely sung song declaring that whatever anybody else in the world does, the farmer is the most important, because he feeds them all. Here, the farmer is the goat, the sucker.

As any "everything's coming up roses" songwriter will tell you, when you're right up against it and haven't a cent, what better than a cheerful song to help you buckle down and look to a brighter future, because it's certainly coming. **You'll Make The Grade Yet** was perhaps a little mis-timed, published as it was some four months before the First World War. At that time the infectious personal boosterism, the moral foundation of every mining town in the West on both sides of the border, was still the creed of every westerner. Similar in tone is the work of the "Lumberman Poet", Douglas Malloch. He started life as a newspaperman and he eventually became a much sought-after inspirational speaker. He was closely connected to the development of the modern myth of Paul Bunyan, and his verses, though full of woods terminology and usually written in a false "workers" style, were full of a homespun cornpone philosophy. His **Possession**, published in the *Star* in 1922, is a good example of the style.

Many of the Irish emigration songs of the 1850's reflected on how Canada and the US did not have aristocrats owning thousands of acres of land, as was common in the old country. The New World was a place for a new start, and many new economic ideas found fertile soil on this side of the Atlantic. A movement of the 1880's, brought into being by the publication of Henry George's *Progress and Poverty*, argued that all taxes on productive labour should be replaced by a single tax -- on land. Those who owned land, who didn't improve it, but who nevertheless made a profit on selling it again, were held to be the worst social parasites, and the sole creators of poverty. If people could use their imagination, skill and drive to make a desert bloom, why should they be taxed? Why not tax the unearned income of land rents? **The System** makes the case in sixteen lines.

A Joyful Sound encapsulates the tone of many of our verses. In four lines it talks about the good things in life, and the best of them all is enough coal in the house on a cold February night.

The Great Depression was triggered in North America by the collapse of stock market prices. The Dow Jones index had peaked 3 September 1929 at 381.17 and then collapsed, finally bottoming out 8 July 1932 at 41.22. It only regained the 1929 peak in 1955. What flowed from this was catastrophic unemployment. Canada's rate was 27% in the depths of the depression in 1933. On top of this industrial collapse came a double hit for the prairies -- agricultural prices collapsed, and the Depression coincided with a long period of drought, where the soil dried up and was blown away, hence the moniker "the dirty thirties."

The Depression did not affect everyone equally. Where some lost their farm, or their job, and had to go on relief, for others, such as Wilfred J. Funk, President of Funk & Wagnalls, the Depression meant debts. We cannot know whether he actually did owe the butcher and the baker, as he claims in his **Merry This and That**.

Remedies for the Depression were many. One response was an increased interest in public ownership, expressed either through the national Communist Parties in Europe or through social democratic parties such as the British Labour Party or Canada's Cooperative Commonwealth Federation (CCF, the forerunner of the NDP). Another response was the growth of nationalist parties, such as the German Nazi party. A third tack was exemplified by such movements as Bill Aberhart's Social Credit party, the proponents of what was popularly called "funny money", or Technocracy, which first saw the light in 1932 and advocated a more rational and productive society headed by technical experts. Our set of verses titled **Technocracy** parodies the Longfellow poem "Excelsior", whose first verse is

> The shades of night were falling fast,
> As through an Alpine village passed
> A youth, who bore, 'mid snow and ice,
> A banner with the strange device,
> Excelsior!

Technocracy borrowed from Taoist philosophy the Taijitu symbol, (a circle divided by a sinous line into two parts, one white and one red) more commonly recognized these days as a symbol of Yin and Yang. This presumably was the "strange device".

In the upper Similkameen, the Depression hit wage earners and business people the hardest. The downturn in the economy caused many workers to be laid off and, with fewer paycheques in the community, businesses suffered. Those affected least were the people who "lived on the land" -- farmers, ranchers and other homesteaders. Martin Grainger who described Princeton during the

Depression in his book *Riding the Skyline* noted that in the upper Similkameen,

> where there are tubs of rich milk cooling in the creek and eggs and surreptitious deer meat, the Depression merely means less money, gasoline and cars to carry people up and down roads unnecessarily.

The song "There's Gold Up in the Tulameen" sums it up by saying:

> Berries for the pickin,' why wander o'er the land?
> There's grouse upon the mountain and deer come to the door
> You're welcome dear old-timer, don't wander any more.

Princeton was also afflicted by another effect of the Depression, which was to drive a wedge between single and married men. Married men had a harder time of it -- they had responsibilities for a family, and all the attendant worries -- was there enough to eat? What if the kids fell sick? Many employers recognized these restraints and when they laid off workers they started with the single men, who, it was reasoned, had less to lose. The pre-1914 Wobblies (the Industrial Workers of the World) had called many married men "the home guard" because it was harder to interest them in thinking or talking about a radical reconstruction of society: they were too busy with their own personal responsibilities. This attitude hardened in the 1930s, and was reflected in Princeton by the writings of an anonymous (but probably male) letter writer who called himself "Martha Muggins". Tongue in cheek, Muggins suggested in a 5 March 1931 letter to the *Similkameen Star*, along the lines of Jonathan Swift's "A Modest Proposal", that since society cared so little for single men, it should arrange for them all to be eliminated. A couple of weeks later, his **A Plea for Single Men** brought about a response in verse from Jay Ell, a regular correspondent and versifier, and the *Star's* stringer in Coalmont. **A Midwinter Night's Dream** imagines the resultant confusion. "Perly" would be Perly Russell, a mainstay of the town, the backbone of the local Conservative Association and a subject of a front-page editorial on his death, and "AOJ" is probably A.O. Johnson, of the Coalmont Hotel. The editor of the paper, Dave Taylor, is also present in the poem, as a well-known town bachelor. The "Martha Muggins/Midwinter Night's Dream" controversy caused such a stir that for weeks afterwards heated letters to the editor on the topic appeared in the *Star.*

Number 4 Tunnel, Blakeburn, 1929. Princeton Museum

Why They Don't Enlist

Ambitious young Americans will not go into the army in these piping times at $16 a month - Army Officer

"What is the plumber makin' now?" said Files-on-Parade;
"A dollar eighty-five an hour," the colour sergeant said.
"What is th' scale f'r layin' brick?" said Files-on-Parade;
"A cent a brick, a cent a brick," the colour sergeant said.
"The carpenter is makin' seven thirty-five a day.
A plasterer can scarcely carry all he makes away,
A farmer gives a farmhand what he wants if he will stay,
An' they're laughin' at the soldier evr'y pay-day."

"What's that a-whizzin' down the street?" said Files-on-Parade;
"A painter's car, a painter's car," the colour sergeant said.
"What's that above so high, so high?" said Files-on-Parade;
"A molder flyin' his balloon," the colour sergeant said.
"There is printers tourin' Europe, an' a-loadin' on their yachts;
"There is boilermakers gamblin' in expensive corner lots;
"There's machinists with their motor-boats that's makin' 30 knots,
An' they're laughin' at the soldier ev'ry pay-day."

Hedley Gazette, 2 January 1908

Try This on Your Clavier

Meat will be cheaper in the spring – news item

The prices that bloom in the spring, tra la
Have nothing to do with the case.
The prices of every old thing, tra la
Are fit for the purse of a king, tra la
So now is the time to erase.
And that's what we mean when we say or we sing
"Oh, bother the prices that bloom in the spring!"
Tra la la la la la
Tra la la la la la
The prices that bloom in the spring!

Coalmont Courier, 20 May 1912

The Average Income

The average income is sorely tried
In the struggle to make ends meet –
To pay the wages of those who help
And the bills for the food we eat.

The cook in the kitchen asks for more
And so does the serving maid.
And then, perforce, as a matter of course,
The increase must be paid.

We are told the coal is about to rise,
The gas bills are twice as large –
And for every strike which threatens the land
The consigner must pay the charge.

So, what are the people going to do
And how are we going to live,
When the average income is stretched and strained
Beyond what it's able to give?

Coalmont Courier, 7 October 1912

Manning Park 1943. The Allan Gill Collection

The Ultimate Victim

The grocer stood in his little store;
He had washed his windows and swept his floor
And he said, "I wonder who'll make a roar
On the cost of things this morning.
No odds what's wrong, and no odds what's right;
My load of worry is never light,
For somebody comes in and wants to fight
On the cost of things each morning.

"These fresh-laid eggs, do you understand,
Were bought and bargained from hand to hand,
And the price went up as the eggs went - and
I am blamed for that this morning.
This flour, this sugar, this bag of salt,
They came by routes that made prices vault;
For the verdict is I am at fault
For the cost of things this morning.

"The people rage and papers howl,
The reformers shout and the voters growl,
And the housewife's face wears a bitter scowl
When she orders things each morning.
Producer, railroad and middleman,
Each makes the product pay all it can
And the folks put me in the roasting pan
For the cost of things each morning."

Coalmont Courier, 5 August 1912

Copper Mountain, ca 1948. Princeton Museum

Heaven's Enough For Him

Last evening I was talking with a grocer old and grey,
Who told me of a dream he had, 'twas just the other day.
While standing in his office, the vision came to view,
For he saw an angel enter dressed in garments white and new.

Said the angel, "I'm from heaven, the Lord just sent me down
To bring you up to glory and put on your golden crown.
You've been a friend to everyone, and worked hard night and day,
You have supported many and from few received your pay,
And we want you up in glory, where you desire to be,
So place your trusting hand in mine and come along with me."

Then the angel and the grocer started up to glory's gate,
But when passing close to Hades, the angel murmured, "Wait!
I have a place to show you – it's the hottest place in hell,
Where the ones that never paid you do in torment always dwell."

And behold! the grocer saw them, his old patrons by the score,
And grabbing up a chair and fan, he wished for nothing more,
But was bound to sit and watch them as they sizzle, singe and burn,
And his eyes would rest on debtors whichever way they'd turn.

Said the angel, "Come on, grocer, there's the pearly gate to see,"
But the grocer only murmured, "This is heaven here for me."

Princeton Star, 17 February 1927

Allenby General Store. Princeton Museum

The Farmer

Living in this community
Are many men of note
And then again, as you will see,
The farmer is the goat.
As every week he comes to town,
You know him by his coat.
He walks the sidewalk up and down,
The farmer is the goat.
We set the price for him to sell
His meat or eggs or oats:
He simply smiles, he knows full well
The farmer is the goat.
He pays the taxes for us all
As all can clearly note,
No matter whether great or small,
The farmer is the goat.
He ploughs the land o'er hill and dell,
In springtime sows his oats,
He never knows if he can sell -
The farmers are the goats.
He raises pigs and beef and sheep,
The butchers loudly gloat,
The farmer is the goat.
They know that they will get them cheap,
The farmer is the goat.
He milks his cows and ships his cream
And to the town doth tote.
The price he gets is just a scream,
The farmer is the goat.
He sells his butter and his eggs
And wears a worn out coat,
And for his pittance fairly begs,
The farmer is the goat.
They watch him go down on the mat
And do not care a groat,
It really is no wonder that
They sometimes get his goat.

They've always kept him down below
While over him they float,
It's nearly time he let them know
He will not be the goat.

Princeton Star, 26 February 1931

You'll Make The Grade Yet

When you're right up against it and haven't a cent.
Going short on the 'eats' and behind with the rent,
And you ask an old friend for a loan and he'll stall,
And you find out too late he was no friend at all,
Don't give up the struggle though coin's hard to get,
Just take hold again and you'll make the grade yet.

Suppose business is dull, or you're out of a job,
Seems you can't get along like the rest of the mob,
And you're blue, and discouraged, and sick of the game,
And the harder you try the result is the same;
Then shake off the blues. It's a tough fight, you bet!
But it can't last forever - you'll make the grade yet.

Then when it's all over and everything's right,
And the clouds are away and the prospects are bright,
And you find out at last that this old earthly ball
Is not such a bad place to live after all,
Don't forget that you once had to scheme and to fret,
But dig in anew, and you'll make the grade yet.

Similkameen Star, 15 May 1914

Possession

There's some of us has this world's goods an' some of us has none
But all of us has got the woods, an' all has got the sun.
So, settin' here upon the stoop, this patch o' pine beside,
I never care a single whoop - fer I am satisfied.
Now, take the pine on yonder hill, it don't belong to me.
The boss he owns the timber – still, it's there fer me to see:
An' 'twixt the ownin' of the same, an' smellin' of its smell,
I've got the best of that there game, an' so I'm feelin' well.
The boss in town unrolls a map an' proudly says, "It's mine,"
But he don't drink no maple sap and he don't smell no pine.
The boss in town he figgers lands in quarter-sections red;
Lord! I just set with folded hands an' breathe 'em in instead.
The boss his forest wealth kin read in cent an' dollar sign;
His name is written in the deed - but all his land is mine.
There's some of us has this world's goods, and some of us has none
But all of us have got the woods, an' all has got the sun.

Princeton Star, 28 July 1922

"Washing Gold in the Streets of Princeton"; a postcard ca.1919. Princeton Museum

The System

When a man has built a barn –
Tax him!
When a man has cleared a farm –
Tax him!
When he lays another roof,
When he grows another hoof,
Hustle 'round and get the proof,
Then tax him!

Has a man some idle earth?
Don't tax him!
Though it's climbing up in worth,
Don't tax him!
Let him reap what others sow,
They are rather chumps, you know!
If they were not they would go
And tax him!

Similkameen Star, 20 October 1916

A Joyful Sound

There's beauty in the thunder's roll
And in the ocean's roar.
I'd rather hear a ton of coal
That hits the basement floor.

Similkameen Star, 22 February 1918

Merry This and That

Now let us give a rousing cheer
That Christmas comes but once a year,
For when I see the Yuletide trees
Along the streets, my thoughts are these –
I owe the taxes, owe the rent,
I owe my broker six per cent,
I owe the butcher, I owe the baker,
Soon I'll owe the undertaker;
Still, I really will not care if
I can only dodge the sheriff!

Princeton Star, 1 January 1931

Hedley stamp mill and slime pond

Technocracy

The price of stocks was falling fast,
As through the great depression passed
A youth who bore, mid howl and whine,
A banner with the magic line,
"Technocracy!"

His brow was high (an all-time height);
His eye was burning Tiger bright;
Of energy, per cap., he sang
And ended with the grand old bang,
"Technocracy!"

"Try not the peak!", the old man said;
"It isn't here – we're in the red!"
The youth held up a staggered chart
And uttered, from his lion heart,
"Technocracy!"

"Oh, stay," the maiden said, "and rest
Thy weary head upon this breast!"
The young man read the market's range,
And sought another social change,
Technocracy!

A traveller by the faithful hound
(Who fed on ticker tape) was found
Buried beneath a giant graph,
But managed at the last to laugh
Technocracy!

Princeton Star, 9 March 1933

A sign on the outskirts of a Depression-era town about meetings of the local technocracy branch

A Plea For Single Men

Editor, *Star*
Princeton, BC
Dear Sir:
Re the unemployment for single men in this district:

When the $20,000,000 was allotted for relief work in Canada was it stated that no single men should be employed in this work? I don't think so. As soon as Copper Mt closed down, within a few days men (married) called a meeting and met the Hon. WA McKenzie [Provincial Minister of Mines] and simply told him they would have work.

Now, as we all know some of these people had been working for years steady with good wages. First class carpenters and machinists when in the ordinary way, if they saw a common pick and shovel man they would look down upon him, but as soon as the crash came along it took the pick and shovel away from the single man and he was told he was not wanted. He cuts no ice at all so he is sent off.

During the years of 1914/18 this same single man was a real man when he was fighting for his king and country. Quite a few of us are still around Princeton and have been for the last 12 years or more.

The only time a single man is any good is when an election is in sight. It would be good for all of us if our minister of mines would see this before the wildcatters come along each year. He should make sure they have enough money to pay for our labour. Every year men working in the district get done out of their hard earned wages and when we report it we are told they have no control over these matters. We, the single men of Princeton and district want work just as much as these family car men.

Who keeps the most parts of Princeton going, the married or single people? Who keeps the restaurants going; who keeps the workingman's hotel going; even the department stores? The single man, after being out to work for a few months, comes in with quite a few dollars – he wants clothes – you don't find him looking through catalogues for some cheap junk -- he goes over to the store and sees what he wants and buys it and pays for it. Not so with the married folks – they send off hundreds of miles away and they buy their stuff and the money they earn in the district is spent with the mail order firm. Take a look any time at the post office and see the goods that Mr. And Mrs. Joe are getting every day from outside. No, the money is good enough to earn here but too good to spend. Some of us have enough sense to know a man can't keep a wife and family – any man working for wages knows this. A man earning $6 per day is spending $6.50. Today you have work, tomorrow the plant closes down.

But what is to become of the single men?

Well the best way to settle the unemployment question is to shoot every single man over the age of 35, Take them all to some waste land or dump and get a firing squad, it will soon be over, and think what a name Princeton would get as the city of the world that has settled the unemployment question for single men.

Yours, etc.
Martha Muggins
Jan 13, 1931

Relief camp for single unemployed men near Whipsaw Creek 1930. Princeton Museum

A Midwinter Night's Dream

'Twas a clear frosty night with the moon shining bright
On the sides of Similkameen valley,
And the crowd gathered there made it look like a fair
Or a scene from an old timers' rally.
Times were hard and 'twas thought to have bachelors shot,
'Twould be stopping a whole lot of bother
And would help out the wives who led strenuous lives
And had trouble in 'bringing up father'.
So they brought bachelors in, short and tall, fat and thin,
Under eagle-eyed married inspectors;
Granite Creek sent a few, and from Tulameen, too,
Came a troop of the old-time prospectors.
Princeton's wifeless brigade was formed up for parade
When our troopers arrived bright and early,
And in looking their way I could see A. O. J.
And the Editor lined up with Perly.
The time speeded on and 'twas nearing the dawn
When a voice hollered, "Bachelors, steady!
Right at five on the dot, the first man will be shot
So fall into line and be ready!"
There ensued quite a din, but I did not fall in,
So a married man started to holler,
But I slid out of bed tangled up in a 'spread,
At the moment he grabbed for my collar.
Now the moral is plain and I'll never again
Find the Muggins' epistles inspiring,
Though they may be quite true, yet they make me feel blue,
And the firing squad nightmares are tiring.

Princeton Star, 19 March 1931

Chapter 12: The Second World War

Like the First World War, the Second World War was a conflict begun in Europe and then joined by most other nations in the world. It might almost be said that there was only one war, which ran from 1914 to 1945, with an intermission for a depression and rearmament. Though the first war was triggered by Austria and was nominally against Serbia (with allies of each joining), its real struggle was Germany vs. the British Empire, Russia and France. The second war featured the same lineup. The only significant change was Italy's alliances: the first war saw her with the Allies, the second with the Nazis. Japan, too, had changed sides.

Unlike the first war, the involvement of Canada in the Second World War arose from a decision made in Canada, seven days after the British ultimatum to Germany had expired. The First World War had automatically included Canada, as a Dominion of the Empire, but the 1931 Statute of Westminster had recognized Canada's sovereignty, and the Canadian Prime Minister had said repeatedly that the Parliament of Canada would decide Canada's actions.

No war mobilized nations as thoroughly as this one did. Worldwide, more than 100 million people were mobilized and every major country devoted their entire apparatus -- scientific, industrial and economic -- towards total victory.

The mobilization of Canada included all the human and material resources of the country. Nothing was wasted, and everything was collected: tin cans became bombers and fighters, paper and fat were recycled. There was also a moral to be drawn: whereas Canadians had had no choice but to sacrifice during the hungry 'thirties, the sacrifice here was to lead to the goal of Victory, and thus was a matter of morale boosting as much as industrial efficiency.

This sentiment is what inspires **For Freedom**, a simple polemic about the need for sacrifice, of service personnel and the "hoarded stores" of Copper Mountain. **Make It Do!** addresses both the factors of efficiency and pride, and **All the Scrap That We've Sent In** makes the further point that sane foreign policies worldwide might have prevented the war in the first place. The fourth of these poems in our collection, **Lay That Pistol Down, Babe and Pick Those Knittin' Needles Up!** is a reworking of a popular song by Al Dexter, now meant to encourage women working through the Red Cross to knit socks, balaclavas and scarves for service people. The 78-rpm release of the original song went to the top of the Billboard Hit Parade just nine weeks before our poem was published.

Wars speed up industrial processes and also engender huge bureaucracies, which are necessary to co-ordinate the plans and actions of millions of people. **Blank Verse** comments wryly on the form-filling such bureaucracy requires.

Modern war also requires vast sums of money, mostly borrowed. War Bonds first saw the light in the American Civil War, and they became an established feature of the Second World War. As "Victory Bonds", they financed about half of Canada's war costs. The earliest sales of War Bonds met their targets immediately, but as the war went on, it was clear that their sale needed promotion. **Somebody's Son**, made by a squadron leader in the RCAF, was one among many such poems that took on the job of maintaining enthusiasm for the raising of the necessary money to carry on the war effort. Another verse on the same theme is **A Stamp A Day Keeps the Japs Away**. The author is not named, but the poem appears in an advertisement in the paper from the Consolidated Mining & Smelting Company of Canada, Limited, better known to us nowadays as Cominco. The company, which owned the fabulously wealthy silver, lead and zinc Sullivan mine at Kimberley, and the smelter at Trail, which transformed the ores into metals, was also one of the main producers of Canadian war material: much of the money raised by War Bond sales would find its way into the company's hands. The most secret project undertaken by them was the production of heavy water for the Manhattan project, which built the first atomic bomb.

So much for the home front -- what about the fighting forces? The Italian campaign of 1943-5 was the first involvement of large numbers of Canadian troops. Some 91,000 Canadians saw service in Italy during those years, and nearly 5,000 were killed there. It is curious that Mussolini, the Italian dictator, more often features in the published verse of the Similkameen than his much more impressive ally, Adolf Hitler. Four of the poems address the international situation, and they are all connected in some way with the Italian campaign.

Operation Husky, the invasion of Sicily, began 10 July 1943. It quickly became clear that the Italian Army was close to collapse, but the German units stationed there fought strongly. Nevertheless, the island was won in 38 days. Mussolini had been deposed 25 July by the Grand Council of Fascism and was arrested the next day. Dorothy Corbett of Merritt celebrates **Mussolini's Fall**: curiously, her poem, published 5 August, doesn't speak of Canada but only of Britain. A poem appearing in a Montreal paper and reprinted locally two weeks later, **Hitler's Conversion**, has him hankering after his old job as a paper-hanger following Mussolini's defeat, and John Robert Mcdonald's **Benito's Lament**, published 26 August, has Mussolini blaming Hitler for not providing more help. Eight days later came the first Canadian landings near Reggio di Calabria, and the much tougher battles that lay ahead.

The next poem, **A Soldier Writes of Italy**, has a curious history. It appeared in the *Similkameen Star* on 2 March 1944, but has appeared in many papers and journals since, sometimes claimed by an author, sometimes by a friend of a named author, but most often as being written by an anonymous soldier. The poem, often titled "A Panorama of Italy", is a curious mixture of tones and registers: wry, disgusted, amused, or saddened, the soldier looks about him at the effects of war and poverty. The poem has an oral origin, since some of the words (in this set, verse 6, line 3 "Moulting", and verse 9, linc 1 "Creysing") are misheard and dis-remembered.

Our final Second World War poem, **The Diner**, appeared 5 October 1944. It contrasts the attention given to a young serviceman in the railway dining car with that given to the same young man who, only a few years before, had "ridden the rods" as a hobo on the same train. Tommy Douglas made the same point in his *The Making of a Socialist*, where he contrasted the ease and speed of Parliament voting $1.5 billion to prosecute the war (15 minutes!) with the days of 1936-1938 where the CCF had "introduced motion after motion asking the government to issue money for the work and wages programme, and had asked for the trifling sum of 500 million dollars. (The) Minister of Finance had looked across at me and said, 'I'd like to tell my young friend that money doesn't grow on gooseberry bushes.' I now had the satisfaction of watching (him) find the gooseberry bush."

For Freedom

The roar of battle sounds across our land,
As ruthless foes press on with cruel hate.
United nations arm with frenzied haste
To stop the mad Beast ere he nears our gate.
Our loved ones go in answer to the call,
With spirits high, they leave their native shores.
We're sending ships and planes and mighty guns,
And Copper Mountain yields its hoarded stores.
Free men we've lived, free men we shall remain
While we've got loyal, gallant sons to send,
To stem the tide of avaricious beasts,
And bring this threat to freedom to an end.

Similkameen Star, 13 August 1942

Make It Do!

Once I had some grand plus fours of splendid Harris tweed
But now, my wife has heard the call and sensed the nation's need.
No longer in those golfing trews I shift the fairway's dirt -
Those well-worn bags, turned fore and aft, are now a lady's skirt.

A dinner jacket once I owned (I hated to get 'dressed')
And as the years increased my weight it strained across my chest.
But now this social slave is free, the needs of war bear fruit,
Those evening clothes have been transformed into a woman's suit.

I had a favourite overcoat - it served me many years,
But she who rules my little roost has sailed in with her shears.
And now a sturdy twelve-year-old is strutting in his pride,
He has a brand-new suit of clothes and walks by daddy's side.

Similkameen Star, 8 April 1943

All The Scrap That We've Sent In

All the scrap that we've sent in
Brings victory to our labours;
But peace will mean that we must scrap
Our scrapping with the neighbours.

Similkameen Star, 19 February 1942

"Lay Those Pistols Down, Babe" And Pick Those Knittin' Needles Up!

I was wearin' army socks, and was I havin' fun,
Until one night they sprung a hole, and now they're on the run.
Pick those needles up, babe, pick those needles up,
Knittin' Purlin' Mama, pick those needles up.

I washed my socks the other day and hung them up to dry,
And when I saw them full of holes I started in to cry.
Pick those needles, up, babe, pick those needles up,
Knittin' Purlin' Mama, pick those needles up.

Flying o'er the sea one day, and I was feelin' cold,
I pulled the helmet on my head and hoped that it would hold.
Get those needles, out, babe, get those needles out,
Knittin' Purlin' Mama, get those needles out.

Across the windy seas sailin' on a battleship,
I wish someone would knit a scarf that would reach down to my toes.
Get those needles out, babe, get those needles out,
Knittin' Purlin' Mama, get those needles out.

The Red Cross needs some workers and needs them every day,
So won't you take a little bit, and help them on their way?
Pick those needles up, babe, pick those needles up,
Knittin' Purlin' Mama, pick those needles up.

Similkameen Star, 27 January 1944

Blank Verse

There's much less rubber for you and me
And much less gas to spill out,
And much less sugar to sweeten tea
But many more forms to fill out.

Forms that ask for your last name first,
Forms that beg for your name reversed,
Forms with pages of printed dope
You couldn't read with a microscope -
Forms to plead for defence priorities,
Forms to mail to the wrong authorities.
Green forms, yellow forms, sky-blue-pink forms,
Please PRINT PLAINLY and please USE INK forms,
Half of them probably out-of-date forms;
FORMS!

There's much less traffic to make us work,
And much less time to take out,
And much less wool for the haggard moth -
But many more blanks to fill out;

Blanks with space you just put X in,
Blanks with your age, height, weight and sex in,
Blanks to swear to and blanks to swear at,
Blanks with blanks that you mustn't write in
Spacious enough to fly a kite in,
And a slot the size of a pygmy flea
For a resume of your history.
Gas blanks, draft blanks, tax blanks, bank blanks,
And just plain blankety-blank-blank-blank, blanks
BLANKS!

Similkameen Star, 23 September 1943

Somebody's Son

Somebody's Son has volunteered to risk his life for you...
Somebody's Son is far from home and the things that homefolk do...
Somebody's Son for your Freedom's sake is preparing himself for War...
Somebody's Son deserves your help for it's YOU he's fighting for!

Somebody's Mother is giving her boy in a Cause that's yours as well...
Somebody's Wife knows a loneliness that only her heart can tell...
Somebody's Mother and Somebody's Wife are doing all they can do...
Somebody prays that some other may care - and the answer is up to YOU!

Somebody's Son in the days to come must meet the bitter Test...
Somebody's Man for our Freedom's plan in a foreign field may rest...
Somebody's Job is to care for them NOW - for on them all our hopes depend...
Somebody's Job is to dig up the cash and that Somebody's YOU, my friend!

Similkameen Star, 26 February 1942

A Stamp a Day Keeps the Japs Away

Two bits, you say - Two bits a day!
I haven't got it to give away.
Just a minute, brother, before you shout,
How much would you give to keep Tojo out?

How much would you give to show him he's wrong?
How much would you give to avenge Hong Kong?

Remember, you're not going to give it away,
It's going to come back on some rainy day,
Some rainy day when your need may be sore;
And you'll wish you'd invested many times more.

Similkameen Star, 6 August 1942

Mussolini's Fall

Stripped of honour, stripped of Empire,
Cringing now before our might,
How the arrogant are fallen:
They who stabbed us in the night.

Backs against the wall, we faced them,
Caught unarmed, in desperate need,
Left alone to overthrow them,
And avenge their cowardly deed.

Overrun was France, and beaten,
Though her heart was loyal still.
Knifed while dying, by Il Duce
And the fiends who did his will.

Now the day of retribution
Dawns for them, his minions all,
Who learned Britain's never beaten
While her back is to the wall.

Similkameen Star, 5 August 1943

Manning Park 1943. The Allan Gill Collection

Hitler's Conversion

Give me back my brush and ladder;
Give me back my paint and paste;
For there's nothing makes me madder
Than a good job gone to waste.

Those were the days when things went swanky,
Those were the days when pay was good;
Now my plans have all gone cranky -
Musso's funked it – Churchill's rude.

Let me once more mix the whiting,
Hang the paper straight and well;
And let Goering do the fighting
And let Goebbels go to hell!

Similkameen Star, 19 August 1943

Benito's Lament

I no likea Adolph, he take all da mon',
He takes all da transports, he take da gun,
He scurry away in da dead of da night,
He leavea no weapon with which I can fight.

Da Allies they come with a shout and a rush;
They mow down my army and makea me blush.
They take my possessions, they're devils to shoot,
And now they blow holes in da toe of da boot.

I no likea Adolph, no likea da Pope;
When I aska for help, they givea no hope.
With all these misfortunes lined up in a row,
Poor Benito's sad, he has no place to go.

Why did I trust Adolph when he tolda me
"I'll give to you Egypt, I'll give you da sea,
King Victor must go and you'll takea his place,
The Pope he is done - you'll wear scarlet and lace."

Poor Benito is sad - his heart's full of pain.
There's guards all around him, he's tied with a chain.
They laugh in his face and his black shirt they tore -
The Allies are here and he'll need it no more.

Similkameen Star, 26 August 1943

Manning Park 1943. The Allan Gill Collection

A Soldier Writes of Italy

If I were an artist with nothing to do
I'd paint a picture, a composite view,
Of historic Italy, in which I'd show
Visions of contrast, the high and the low.

There'd be towering mountains, a deep blue sea.
Filthy brats yelling "Caramella!" at me.
High plumed horses and colourful carts,
Two-toned tresses on hustling tarts.

I'd show Napoleonic cops, the Carabinieri,
Dejected women with too much to carry,
A dignified gent with a balboa beard,
Bare-bottomed bambinos, both ends smeared.

Castle and palace, opera house too,
Hotel on a mountain, marvellous view.
Homes made of weeds, brick and of mud,
People covered with scabs, scurvy and crud.

Chapels and churches great to behold,
Each a king's ransom in glittering gold.
Poverty and want, men craving for food,
Picking through garbage, practically nude.

Stately cathedrals with high-toned bells.
Ricover shelters with horrible smells,
Mouldy catacombs, a place for the dead,
Noisy civilians clamouring for bread.

Political villas with palm trees tall,
A stinking hovel, mere hole in the wall.
Tree-fringed lawns swept by the breeze,
Goats wading in filth up to their knees.

Big breasted damsels but never a bra,
Bumping against you, there should be a law.
Revealing statues, all details complete,
A sensual lass with sores on her feet.

Creysing boulevards, a spangled team,
Alleys that wind like a dope fiend's dream.
Flowers blooming on the side of a hill,
A sidewalk latrine with privacy nil.

Barbers galore with manners quite mild,
Prolific women, all heavy with child.
Il Duce's secret weapon, kids by the score
Caused by a bonus which is no more.

Arrogant wretches, picking up snipes,
Miniature Fiats, various types,
A beauteous maiden, a smile on her face
With a breath of garlic fouling the place.

Families dining from one common bowl
Next to the fish stores, a horrible hole.
Italian zoot-suiters, flashily dressed,
Bare-footed beggars looking depressed.

Mud-smeared children clustering about,
Filling their jugs from a community spout.
A dutiful mother with a look of despair
Picking the lice from her small daughter's hair.

Capable craftsmen skilled in their art,
Decrepit old shacks, falling apart.
Intricate needlework out on display
Surrounded by filth, rot and decay.

I've tried to describe the things that I've seen;
Panorama of Italy, the brown and the green.
I've neglected the war scars visible yet
But those are the things we want to forget.

I'm glad I came, but damned anxious to go -
Give it back to the natives, I'm ready to blow.

Similkameen Star, 2 March 1944

The Diner

He was dining on the diner; and the waiter called him "Sir":
White linen decked his table and gleaming silverware.
They placed good food before him, he sat and ate his fill;
They paid him every service and his country paid the bill.
And he thought of another journey of a not far distant date,
When he passed through this same country, just a hobo on a freight.
His country did not need him, for he had no work to do
And he wore no service uniform of khaki, or of blue.
When his grim task is over, perhaps we'll understand
That hungry mouths may all be fed from the plenty of our land.

The Similkameen Star, 5 October 1944

Number 1 Shaft Headframe, Copper Mountain Mine. Princeton Museum

Chapter 13: A Pot Pourri of Topical Verses

- a collection of verses from valley newspapers over the first half of the 20th century, with no common theme save that of not falling naturally into a theme.

OU PARSON

The "Parson" referred to in this verse is Reverend George Wilson from Scotland, Parson of the Presbyterian Church in Coalmont in 1912. His departure from this congregation at the end of September of 1912 after only five months of service and his farewell sermon 29 September caused a minor tempest in the town. Excerpts from his sermon were published in the *Coalmont Courier* 30 September 1912. A sample follows.

- Your commercial Association started out with a big beating of drums and unfurling of flags, and in a few weeks' time it all fell flat – there's not a businessman amongst you.

- The myth of Jonah and the whale would be scoffed at by the present day schoolboy. A mammal with a throat only large enough to take in a man's arm is stated to have swallowed Jonah, who stayed inside for three days and subsequently went on his way rejoicing.

- There are only two men in the room who can give offhand a definition of the word money – I'm one of them [hope we are the other one, though we don't often get enough of it to define. – Ed.] –yet you profess to know your business.

- You fellows don't believe in ghosts or fairies or goblins, but if you heard a noise in the brush after dark you would shin up the nearest tree trunk. You certainly can't know much if you lay out a kegful of molasses to trap a bear.

- What is the definition of a hero? A Mormon

A week later the poem **OU Parson** was published in the *Courier* together with a letter entitled "A Dig at the Parson" from "No Knocker" and a promise from the editor that the following week would feature a response from the Parson to the criticism leveled at him. "No Knocker" begins by referring to the "wild utterances of our very obviously ossified oddity, viz., Reverend George Wilson." "No Knocker" objects to Wilson's "insolence regarding the ignorance of us common followers [which] shows plainly his opinion of all others." He concludes by advising Wilson that "if he would get along in this country he had better hunt a little for some of what is commonly called 'horse sense' and molasses is no bait to use to get it."

The following week the paper published " Wilson Slashes Coalmonter – The following extraordinary panegyric from the Rev. Geo. A. Wilson, LL.B., fell into the *Courier* mailbag Saturday night and is reproduced after some expurgations...." At one point the *Courier's* editor inserts ["Too personal, George, got to kill this page"]. Wilson's letter calls "No Knocker" a "lubbering pinhead" and runs for several pages attacking his spelling, grammar and ignorance. Wilson goes so far as to say "Some day they may enclose you in an insane asylum or a museum of natural freaks." He finishes with a warning: "I know you, Sir Knocker, but I want to make sure of you, so sign your name. Then bear in mind that I never forget a friend nor forgive a foe!" -- a rather un-Christian stance for a man of the cloth. Whatever it was that alienated the Reverend Wilson from his congregation, he was certainly burning his bridges before he departed. On the copy of the *Coalmont Courier* we read in the Princeton Archives containing "OU Parson" someone had handwritten an extra last line to the poem; "Who thinks Clark is an ass? We all do." One wonders whether Clark is the secret identity of "No Knocker."

O U Parson!

Who said that Coalmont streets were paved with gold?
The Parson.
Who said that souls on earth were bought and sold?
The Parson.
Who said that Coalmont's business men were stale?
The Parson.
Who said that Jonah swallowed the whale? The Parson.
Who invented primarily the dollar bill? The Parson.
Who only knoweth how the bear to kill? The Parson.
Who at the gallant Coalmont hunters strikes? The Parson.
Who is it says he black molasses likes? The Parson.
Who was so highly jealous of the bear? The Parson.
Who thinks it gobbled up the bigger share? The Parson.
Who came across from Bonnie Scotland dear? The Parson.
Who came to study ignorance up here? The Parson.
Who is it acts the part of uncouth churl? The Parson.
Who so stands in with nary pretty girl? The Parson.
Who thinks that heroes are of Mormon breed? The Parson.
Who wishes he belonged unto their creed? The Parson.
Who likes his knowledge of long words to air? The Parson.
Who thinks for satire he can skill Voltaire? The Parson.
Who thinks that he can ride a fiery steed? The Parson.
Who thinks the world lies north the Banks of Tweed?
The good old Parson.

Coalmont Courier, 7 October 1912

Princeton Train Station. Princeton Museum

The Lone Grouse Supper

Two weeks after Reverend Wilson's letter was published, the Coalmont Courier ran these verses. It describes a loaves-and-fishes-style meal where a single grouse "feeds" ten people. We thank Coalmont historian Diane Sterne for information about the characters in this poem. "Fred, the man of poolroom fame" mentioned in the third line is Fred Lawney who operated Gabe's Pool Room in Coalmont. "Pringle", the practical joker who supplied the grouse, owned a livery barn in Coalmont and was a partner in the firm, Budd Pringle and Shae. "Al", described as "the parson's foeman", is likely Al Dashwood, a Coalmont businessman whom Diane describes as having "his hand in pretty much everything in town". Diane suspects that Ed Clark wrote this poem. Clark, who was apparently not well liked, was run out of town by magistrate C.E. Thomas in 1914.

The Lone Grouse Supper

[The poetical Coalmont Chef invited a few friends to a "grouse dinner" one evening last week, prior to his departure for the Coast. The menu consisted of one small bird. —Ed.]

One day about a week ago,
A bunch of Coalmonters, you know,
Were asked up to the Coalmont House
To eat a feed of 'Pringle' grouse.
First Fred, the man of poolroom fame
And Al, the parson's foeman, came;
Joe, who hunts the bears so well,
And with him came his sister Nell;
Hal the Jew, and Katie, too,
The only absent one was Hugh;
Miss Burgess, Coalmont's latest guest
And then came Pringle to the fest;
The 'Coalmont Chef" who cooked the grouse,
And William from the printing house.
The board all set, the guests await
With hungry eyes fixed on each plate
Till time the crucial moment brings
With it the grouse on red-hot wings.

A breathless silence now pervades
This feast of youthful men and maids
Eight or nine sharp eyes or more
Now turn towards the kitchen door,
When out there comes Missouri Slim
All deck-ed out in waiter's trim
Bewaring on gigantic plate
The fowl for which they'd had to wait.
On he comes with stately mien,
Toes turned in and smile serene.
At last the platter down he set
And swift and silent made his get.
When lo behold one fearsome grouse
No bigger than a full-grown mouse!
Consternation then there sat
And faces thin and faces fat,
Questioning glances darted round
And presently the answer found:
The group, though formed of witty folk,
Were made the victims of a joke!
Just for a moment blank display
Gave place to looks which had been gay
But Coalmont people are good sorts
And take their medicine like sports
And so, with jest and laughter free
Were soon as merry as could be
Determined they would make the best
Of what as offered at the fest
The bird was passed along to Nell
Who carved it up and did it well,
Everybody had a share,
So after all they didn't care.
Instead of grouse they had to make
Their dinner out of tea and cake;
For dessert each had licorice pipe,
And all the toothpicks he could swipe;
Some candy, too, helped swell the fare,
And lots of chewing gum was there
So after all 'twas not so bad,
And not a single one was mad,

As homeward on their way they went
And at the store some money spent
To buy the makings of a feed
To satisfy their stomachs' need.
Joe Wigmore says for many a day
The joke will surely be the way
How ten young people hale and strong
Sat down and ate for two hours long
Around a platter filled with grouse
No bigger than a full-grown mouse.

"Chirping Charlie"
Coalmont Courier, 28 October 1912

Ode(ius) Spring

This verse was likely written by Peck McSwain, an itinerant printer mentioned frequently and affectionately in the *Star* during the 1920s. The poet appears to be suffering from spring fever, which makes him "want to work no more". In the second stanza, he compares himself with Walt Mason, the Kansas newspaperman known as the "poet laureate of American democracy" and whose poetry became so well known that he was familiarly known as "Uncle Walt". Harold Teen, also mentioned in stanza two, was the main character of a popular, long-running American comic strip of the same name that ran from 1919 to 1959. It was written and drawn by Carl Ed.

The poet expresses feeling pressure to "hustle to beat that Coalmont guy, Ell - Jay". "Jay Ell", who published numerous poems in the paper, was the pseudonym used by the *Princeton Star's* correspondent from Tulameen and Coalmont.

The "sedans and open cars" referred to in stanza four have been dug from their "lairs" because the melting snow in April makes driving possible again. The license plates adorning the cars are "new" because it was only in the 1920s that license plates began being issued through sub-offices throughout the province. Before that vehicles were registered directly with the Motor Vehicle Branch in Victoria.

In the week that this poem was published, Princeton was voting in a plebiscite under the "Village Municipalities Act" (stanza six) to determine whether it would remain as an unorganized district or become a municipality. Those who were "staging quite a fight" were those opposing incorporation and who had distributed a leaflet entitled "Real Property Owners of Princeton" just before the plebiscite. Their arguments against incorporation revolved around increased taxes and liability:

> Can we afford to have improvements which will increase our taxes?....Who would have to pay the damages of any law suit?

Stanza six also mentions prohibition in the United States. In January 1920, the US went dry and breweries, distilleries and saloons closed their doors. By 1927 when this poem was published, prohibition was far from "tight". Americans had found many ways to get around the law. That same year, Al Capone's Chicago bootlegging organization reportedly took in $60 million and had half the city's police on its payroll.

Ode(ius) Spring

I ain't been feeling right this week,
Nor yet the week before;
There's somthin' in the air what makes
Me want to work no more.

I see Walt Mason's off his oats,
And so is Harold Teen,
And Mournful Mike says nowadays
Ain't what they uster been.

I guess it is the budding trees
And green grass shouting spring;
And buzzin' bees and singin' birds
That make the welkin ring.

And the grand sedans and open cars,
And e'en the homemade bug,
Resplendent with new licence plates,
That from their lairs are dug.

The salesman of the brand new car
Brings forth his line of bunk,
And tells you that your good old bus
Is nothing but mere junk.

The Princeton folks on the "Village Act"
Are staging quite a fight;
And the States declare they're going to make
Old prohibition 'tight'.

And spring sales are the usual thing
In nearly every store,
With windows draped in suits and hats
And dresses by the score.

I guess the spring air's in my blood,
But I have said enough,
I want to keep on writing but
I'd fill this page with stuff.

It's seldom that I want to write
Meanderings in this way,
And I'll have to hustle it I want to beat
That Coalmont guy, Ell - Jay!

"Mac"
Princeton Star, 7 April 1927

The Spanish Flu

The Spanish flu of 1918 was an unusually severe and deadly epidemic that spread across the world and lasted from June 1917 to December 1920. Some 500 million were infected and an estimated 50 to 100 million people died worldwide, making it one of the deadliest natural disasters in history. Most victims were healthy young adults. The First World War with its close quarters hastened the spread of the disease. Increased travel and massive troop movements facilitated the worldwide occurrence of the flu -- modern transportation systems made it easier for soldiers, sailors and other travelers to spread the disease.

News of this worldwide killer must have frightened people in the Similkameen valley, which makes the jocular tone of **The Flu**, published in January of 1919 while the epidemic was still raging, all the more astonishing. It's another example of a stance that shows itself in many of these poems -- fortitude and a sense of humour in the face of adversity.

The Spanish flu was first mentioned in the *Similkameen Star* 25 October 1918. At that time there were 8 cases of the flu in the area, mostly out of town. By 1 November this had risen to over 60. Penticton had 5 cases, Vernon 75, Kelowna 50 and Merritt over 30. By 8 November there were over 100 cases in and around Princeton, of whom 8 had died. A week later there were 6 more deaths and a few new cases. By 29 November the flu ban on poolrooms, theatres, churches, lodges and schools had been lifted and organizations resumed regular meetings. The *Star* reported 26 deaths to date in Princeton and Allenby and 400 cases altogether. The percentage of deaths was apparently lower than in other places. On 6 December there was one death and a week later the *Star* stated that the epidemic was disappearing, because it was the first week with no deaths and no new cases. The *Star* of 3 January 1919 describes a Chinese "cure" for flu and at the end of the month announces a ban on dancing decreed by the provincial government.

This poem is by American writer J.P. McEvoy (1897-1958) and was also published in his 1919 book, *Slams of Life.*

The Flu

When your back is broke and your eyes are blurred,
And your shinbones knock and your tongue is furred,
And your tonsils squeak and your hair gets dry,
And you're doggone sure that you're going to die,
But you're skeered you won't and afraid you will,
Just drag to bed and have your chill,
For you've got the flu, boy; you've got the flu.

When your toes curl up and your belt goes flat,
And you're twice as mean as a Thomas cat,
And life is a long and a dismal curse,
And your food all tastes like a hard-boiled hearse,
When your lattice aches and your head's a-buzz,
And nothing is as it ever wuz,
Here are my sad regrets to you,
For you've got the flu, boy; you've got the flu.

What is it like, this Spanish Flu?
Ask me, brother, for I've been thru.
It is my Misery out of Despair,
It pulls your teeth and curls your hair,
It thins your blood and braise your bones,
And fills your craw with moans and groans,
And sometimes maybe, you get well,
Some call it flu; I call it hell.

Similkameen Star, 3 January 1919

Tale Of The Spanish Flu

This poem is based on the nursery rhyme, "Ten Little Indians", where with each line something happens to one of the Indians until the last line, "And then there were none". "The Tale of the Spanish Flu" begins with twenty nurses working at the Royal Inland Hospital who by the eleventh line are reduced to "eight poor bewildered nurses." They are not, however, reduced to "none" because they are joined by scores of "brave volunteers". The volunteers who proclaim their immunity at the end of the poem credit the "four-ply cheese cloth mask" ordered by the doctor as the agent of their survival. In 1919, when this poem was published, the use of facemasks as a protection against contagion was fairly new. It was only in 1918 that the British Medical Journal published an article about the "prophylactic face mask", and even hygienic hand washing was a relatively recent practice.

The Tale Of The Spanish Flu at Royal Inland Hospital, Kamloops

Twenty gallant nurses working in their blue,
"Clip" took an awful cold, Dr. called it Spanish Flu;
Nineteen doubtful nurses, wondering if 'twas right.
"Mac's" got a red nose which proves this statement quite.
Eighteen frightened nurses charmed to do their best--
Out came a bottle labelled 'Gargle - T.I. d. h. s.'
They gargled, and they sprayed for seven days or more,
But their efforts they were fruitless, some more must leave the floor.
It happened Thursday morning when ten more began to sneeze;
Before the week was ended, the East wing boasted these.
Eight poor bewildered nurses, they flew around like mad,
But not long, before nightfall, brave volunteers they had.
They came in groups of ten or more, like soldiers to a fight,
And willing hands soon made the Wards look neat, and clean and white.

And then an order from the Doc came, he firmly wished to ask
That we keep our noses covered with a four-ply cheesecloth mask;
And when we sneeze, sneeze in our masks, and when we're coughing too,
To keep the germs well under and thus end the Spanish Flu.
So soon we'll all be better, and we'll sing a lively tune,
To the R. I. H. forever, we're immune, yes, we're immune.

M. Hawthorne
T.I.d.h.s. Tincture of iodine daily at night
Princeton Star, 20 January 1919

The Women's Institute

The Women's Institute, whose motto is "For Home and Family", describes itself as an "Educational Organization for Women and Families". It was founded in Ontario in 1897 and by 1909 the organization had spread to British Columbia, where fifteen different Institutes in various rural communities provided care for the elderly, visits to shut-ins, assistance for the ill or bereaved or help to families in time of special need. In 1911, the British Columbia Agricultural Assistance Act was passed, which gave legal recognition to the Institutes. In addition to the services mentioned above, the Institute also organized and funded some of the earliest public washrooms and their efforts were crucial in the establishment of many hospitals, libraries and community halls. Like today's food banks, or like the Parent Advisory Committees in schools today who hold bake sales to raise money for such things as field trips or library books, the Women's Institute provided facilities and services needed by the community which were either under-funded or not provided by the government. Their activities were likely the example as well as the impetus for the provision of many government services.

The second stanza of the verse mentions the women's franchise. Women in BC won the right to vote after long and contentious struggles spearheaded by the Women's Christian Temperance Union (WCTU), a strong advocate for women's suffrage as well as for prohibition. Its members believed that if women were enfranchised, they would vote overwhelmingly for prohibition. They were influenced by the social gospel movement, which held that creating the right social conditions would bring an end to alcoholism, crime and other social problems. The Women's Institute was involved in exactly this kind of work. The struggles of the WCTU resulted in the Provincial Election Act Amendment of 1917, which extended the provincial franchise to women, and the British Columbia Prohibition Act.

There was a branch of the Women's Institute in Keremeos in the early 1920s and the publication of this poem in the *Princeton Star* shows that there was awareness of the organization throughout the valley. The poem, with lines such as "...we love them all but, hang it, they're too cute" demonstrates a patronizing attitude towards "uppity" women who meddle in the public world that is run by men. As if to emphasize that women's place is in the kitchen, the editor of the *Star* places the poem among articles about "Canning Without Sugar," "Canning Peas" and "Eleven Things to Remember When Baking a Cake".

Keremeos Women's Institute, 1921. Penticton Museum

The Women's Institute

We've got our staid commissions, our Guilds and Parties too,
We've got whole rafts of unions; each year there's something new
We've got our Liberal government; they're mighty smart but - Shoo!
Its hopeless work for men to buck The Women's Institute.

The female we've known to be more deadly than the male
And since they got the franchise, Friend, they've got us by the tail.
The privilege they captured then proved such a mighty boost,
The men have 'beat it' for the woods and women rule the roost.

And now to prove our statement that they can't be ignored,
We'll tell of how Victoria crossed their advis'ry board
And chaos reigned throughout the land, the women would not rest -
The government got tangled with a real live hornet's nest.

And things grew pretty hot, you bet, from here to Timbuctoo;
Mere man was quickly put to rout - soon learned a thing or two.
And did they win? Of course they did - we dare not dare deny it
No man with sense would risk their wrath, now that they're home and quiet.

And so the old world wags along. We progress on our way.
The women long deserved to vote - they show it every day,
God bless their souls! We love them all but, hang it, they're too cute.
They beat, us to it when they formed that Women's Institute.

W.C Moteley
Princeton Star, 3 September 1920

Allenby School, c. 1940. Princeton Museum

Dominion Day

These verses were published in honour of the upcoming Dominion Day celebrations on 1 July 1923. Dominion Day, now called Canada Day or "Canada's Birthday", has been celebrated continuously in the Similkameen valley since the early years of the twentieth century. The day's program followed a similar pattern from year to year -- horse races, baseball, athletic events and contests -- with a dance in the evening to crown the day's activities. The 1929 celebration even featured a first aid contest.

Dominion Day marks the joining of the British colonies of Nova Scotia, New Brunswick and the Province of Canada (comprising Upper and Lower Canada) into a federation under the British crown on 1 July 1867. Dominion Day began in 1868 with a royal proclamation by Governor General the Viscount Monck asking Canadians to celebrate the anniversary of Confederation. The holiday was not officially recognized until 1879 when Parliament designated it as Dominion Day. No official national celebrations were held until 1917, the 50th anniversary of Confederation, and then again ten years later. The people of the Similkameen valley, however, have celebrated the occasion annually since the turn of the century.

Even though Dominion Day was a national celebration, many people in this country during the early 20th century viewed themselves not so much as Canadian but as part of the British Empire. Songs with lyrics such as "The Empire is our country and Canada our home" were taught in schools. The Canadian flag until 1965 was the Red Ensign, which featured the Union Jack in the upper left-hand corner. "God Save the Queen" was Canada's national anthem until 1980. Even in the Similkameen valley, over 10,000 kilometers from the "Motherland", this mentality was prevalent. The advertisement in the *Similkameen Star* for the 1912 Dominion Day celebrations speaks of "Our King, One Flag, One People". The 27 June 1929 *Princeton Star* describes the Dominion Day celebrations as having been advertised "from Land's End to John O'Groats", a reference to British rather than Canadian geography.

The tone of **Dominion Day** is in marked contrast to the quotidian, often ribald tone of much of the verse in this book. Instead of Bill and Sam cursing the weather and the "lousy grub", we get a personified Canada, which "enthroned,...wields a righteous way". We can visualize Bill and Sam in their primitive cabin in the bush but what does Canada, "Great in her firmness of intent" look like? The poem is somewhat reminiscent of the version of "O Canada" by Robert Stanley Weir that was published in an official form for the Diamond Jubilee of Confederation in 1927 and which became the accepted version of the national anthem in English-speaking Canada. Where "O Canada" speaks of "true patriot love" and "glowing hearts, "Dominion Day" speaks of "loyal love" and "sturdy hearts". Nineteenth and early twentieth century patriotism was typically couched in such abstract language. It is, in fact the language of hymns that often speak of love and honour to God rather than to country:

> We love the place, O God,
> Wherein thine honor dwells;
> The joy of thine abode
> All earthly joy excels.

Patriotism and loyalty to the church were sentiments that closely resembled one another. In 18th century France, for example, it

Allenby Flotation Mill. Princeton Museum

was argued that clerics should not be allowed to teach in public schools as their *patrie* was heaven, so that they could not inspire love of the homeland in their students.

It is appropriate here to draw a distinction between patriotism and nationalism. Nationalism is not necessarily an inherent part of patriotism. The *Oxford English Dictionary* defines a patriot as "one who disinterestedly or self-sacrificingly exerts himself to promote the well-being of his country". Nationalism is defined as "the doctrine that certain nations are the object of divine election". Nationalism can thus include the belief that one state is naturally superior to other states. This exclusionary quality is epitomized by British Columbia's provincially "nationalistic" motto, "The Best Place on Earth". In this context nationalism isn't so much a sentiment as a marketing strategy.

Patriotism focuses more on abstract values such as freedom, honour, glory or love. We would argue that the songs and poems about Canada from the 19th and early 20th centuries are patriotic rather than nationalistic for precisely this reason. "The Maple Leaf Forever" speaks of being "joined in love together"; in "O Canada" the country is described as "glorious and free." **Dominion Day** fits into this pattern perfectly when it speaks of Canada as being "Destined to fill a purpose vast".

Similkameen Star,
19 June 1912

Dominion Day

T he fair Dominion holds this
H er festival of high esteem;
E nthroned she wields a righteous sway.

G reat in her firmness of intent
R esourceful, by her wealth of lands,
E ach year expands her growing might;
A nd sturdy hearts and willing hands
T hus frame her sovereignty of right.

D estined to fill a purpose vast,
O ur country shall her soul reveal;
M ay those who treasure still the past
I n loyal love her welfare feel.
N ow shape the days of grand emprise,
I n trenchant deeds her sons are famed;
O n seaward wings her spirits rise,
N or shall her freedom now be tamed.

W.G. Boynton
Princeton Star, 29 June 1923

Sister Kittie

An appropriate subtitle for this poem might be "Home Economics Meets Mother's Kitchen". From our early 21st century perspective, we take an awareness -- if not a knowledge -- of nutrition and hygiene for granted. When this poem was published such awareness was relatively new. The first vitamin complexes were isolated in the early 1910s and the word "vitamin" was not commonly used until the 1920s.

The notion of actually studying nutrition and household management emerged in the US in the 1860s with the introduction of domestic science courses at universities. The term "Home Economics" was coined at a conference of academics in Lake Placid,

New York, in 1899. This conference laid the groundwork for the establishment of the American Home Economics Association in 1909 as well for the introduction of courses in Home Economics at schools, colleges and universities not only in the US but throughout North America. Sister Kittie has obviously taken some of these courses at college.

The author of this piece isn't known but it was published in other North American newspapers in 1913. The fact that it was published locally suggests that discussions around nutrition and hygiene, even in the remote Similkameen valley, had already moved from the home into the public arena.

Sister Kittie

Sister Kittie's home from college with a host of modern kinks
In the way of hygienics, sanitation, food and drinks.
Proteids and carbohydrates she combines exactly right,
For the strictly balanced ration she identifies at sight.
She knows all about digestion, what is best for us to eat;
What we need for bodybuilding, growth and force, repair and heat;
And the dinner table's lovely when my sister has it set
But we haven't lost our confidence in mother's cooking yet!

Similkameen Star, 13 June 1913

Shem Ham And Japhet

We first met Shem, Ham and Japhet in the Settlement chapter where they were longing to be in a warmer climate. In this poem, also written by Jay Ell, they comment on the Coué method of autosuggestion, a fad that was popular at the time. Émile Coué was a French psychologist and pharmacist who wrote *Self-Mastery Through Conscious Autosuggestion.* Coué's methodology, which included a mantra-like motto to be repeated regularly, "Day by day, in every way, I'm getting better and better", was based on the principle that any idea that exclusively occupied the mind turned into reality. His book came out in North America in 1922, a year before this poem was published, and his ideas were adopted and spread across the continent. It was featured in Budd Schulberg's novel *What Makes Sammy Run?*, a rags-to-riches story chronicling the rise and fall of Sammy Glick, a Jewish boy born in New York's Lower East Side, who very early in his life makes up his mind to escape the ghetto and climb the ladder of success.

It is interesting to speculate how Coué's autosuggestion technique found its way to the wilds of the upper Similkameen. Shem, Ham and Japhet, like the characters in Jay Ell's "Sam's Supper Soliloquy", are Tulameen bachelors who are ostensibly using autosuggestion to go skating and to stop drinking – unlikely pursuits for men of their type. The pun at the end of the poem – "as he hit the hay…sounds like bunk" -- sums up their (and Jay Ell's) attitude towards Coué's method.

Shem, Ham and Japhet

Said Shem, "I like to skate each day;
It helps to give me vim,
And day by day in every way,
I feel in better trim."

Said Ham, "With 'skates' I went astray
But now the booze I ban,
And day by day in every way,
I feel a better man."

Said Japhet, as he hit the hay,
"What fools we mortals be;
This 'day by day in every way'
Sure sounds like bunk to me."

Princeton Star, 2 February 1923

Coronation Preparations

This poem appeared at a time when Canada was part of the British Empire. Canadian citizens were British subjects and in the early years of the century many of them, especially those of British origin, maintained a strong identification with Britain. "God Save the King" was the national anthem and the song "The Empire is our Country and Canada is our Home" was part of the British Columbia school music curriculum. The majority of the population in the Similkameen valley at this time was of British origin and the coronation of a new King would have been an event of great interest and significance to them.

King Edward VII was the eldest son of Queen Victoria, born in 1841. At her death 22 January 1901 he was thus 61. The coronation was originally scheduled for 26 June 1902, but Edward had to undergo an emergency appendectomy operation, so the coronation was postponed until 9 August 1902. *Coronation Preparations* appeared in the *Similkameen Star* two weeks before the event.

The poem first appeared in the *Portland Oregonian* and was thus most likely written by an American. In fact, in the first stanza, it calls on two renowned American journalists to cover the coronation.

Richard Harding Davis was a journalist and writer of fiction and drama, known for his flamboyant style and his writing on controversial subjects such as abortion, suicide and execution. In April 1902, he was in Martinique in the Caribbean covering the eruption of Mount Pelée. The poem also suggests that William Albert White, a renowned author and newspaper editor from Emporia, Kansas, be brought in to "take the British journalist and show him how to write".

In the third line the poem suggests that Rudyard Kipling memorialize the coronation. Kipling, however, was raising money for the troops and reporting for army publications on the Boer War that was raging at the time. He spent two weeks in Bloemfontein where he came face to face with the "dogs of war" -- deaths from battle, typhoid and dysentery and appalling conditions in the barracks.

Events such as coronations were typically memorialized by Britain's poet laureate. The poem takes a dig at the then-current poet laureate, Alfred Austin, by suggesting that he buy a "rhyming dictionary", "scented notepaper" and "tinted ink". The appointment of Austin was, in fact, controversial, the suggestion being that his appointment had much to do with his position as an editor and leader writer, his friendship with Lord Salisbury the prime minister and his willingness to use his poetry to support the government. Shortly before his appointment was announced, for example, Austin published a sonnet entitled *A Vindication of England*, written in response to a series of sonnets by William Watson that had accused Salisbury's government of betraying Armenia and abandoning its people to the Turks.

William Waldorf Astor, mentioned at the beginning of the third stanza, was a very wealthy American who eventually became a British nobleman. He was a member of the prominent Astor family and upon the death of his father in early 1890 inherited a personal fortune that made him the richest man in America. He moved to Britain in 1891 and became a British subject in 1899. His copious donations to charities in Britain earned him a peerage in 1916. At the time of King Edward's coronation he was still only a rich American with a wannabe British accent and "a coronet of diamonds worth ten million" who was interested in gaining British social distinction.

In the early decades of the 20th century the songs and poems about Britain and Canada that appeared in Similkameen valley newspapers -- such as **Dominion Day** that appears earlier in this chapter -- were typically serious and patriotic. This poem, on the other hand, makes fun of the pomp and ceremony of the coronation, referring to the inclusion of the "Lord of the Coal Cellar", the "Curator of Dachshunds", "Princess Blank" and "Lady This" in the event. The perspective is a western American one; the layers of history and protocol involved in the coronation would have appeared in the New World to be overdone and foppish. It would be interesting to know whether the editor of the *Similkameen Star* who published this poem in the paper shared that point of view.

Coronation Preparations

Bring back Richard Harding Davis
From unsteady Martinique,
Where he's writing up Mont Pelée
For a thousand bones a week;
Call off Kipling from his lashing
Of the backward dogs of war,
Train him down, until he's equal
To his record speed once more;
Buy a rhyming dictionary
For the laureate to read,
Get the scented pink notepaper
And the tinted ink he'll need;
Hale from out the wilds of Kansas
Mr. William Allen White,
Who can take the British journalist
And show him how to write;
Line them up, with pad and pencil,
In a glittering array,
For without them you can never have
A coronation day.

Get the Lord of the Coal Cellar
And the Keeper of the Snakes,
And the Lord High Grand Past Master
Of the Shovels, Hoes and Rakes.
Bring the Curator of Dachshunds
And the Master of the Goats,
And the Lord High Head Inspector
Of the Royal Overcoats;
Take the Reverend High Butcher
And the Honoured Grocery Man.

And the Honorary Keeper
Of the Palace Coal Oil Can,
Tog them out in robes of honor
That it took ten years to make,
With trainbearers by the hundred
Marching proudly in their wake.
Stand them up to make the borders
Of the wide and rose-strewn way,
Which will lead unto the palace
On glad coronation day.

Mr. William Waldorf Astor,
With his accent, will be there,
With a coronet of diamonds
Worth ten million on his hair,
Princess Blank and Duchess Dashleigh,
Lady This and Madam That,
Each in jewel-set tiara
Or an acre picture hat,
All in gowns well calculated
To make every other dame
Scorch and wither up in envy's
Cruel, all-consuming flame.
Give them place in all their glory
When the great parade goes by,
Let their splendor fill with beauty
Every wonder-stricken eye,
And when you have got together
All that marvelous array,
Well, perhaps, you'll need King Edward
On the coronation day.

Similkameen Star, 26 July 1902

Trouble On The Similkameen

A Provincial Election was held in BC 2 February 1907. In the Similkameen riding, the two candidates were Lytton Wilmot Shatford, a Hedley merchant, running for the governing Conservative Party and Smith Curtis, a mining operator in Rossland, running for the Liberals. The *Hedley Gazette*, where this poem was published, supported Shatford, and the *Similkameen Star* supported Curtis. When Shatford spoke in Hedley the *Gazette's* headline was "A Rousing Meeting -- Shatford Gets Hearty Greeting" and when Curtis spoke in Keremeos the *Star's* headline was "In Favour of Curtis". The poem is generally self-explanatory except for the mention of a few names. "Dunc" in the fifth stanza is Duncan Ross, the federal Liberal MP for Yale-Cariboo and "McInnis" in the penultimate stanza is William B. McInnes, the federal Liberal MP for Alberni, both of whom were supposedly sent to BC by Liberal Prime Minister Wilfred Laurier to boost the provincial party's campaign.

MARK 'EM LIKE THIS

And You Will Be Voting for Your Own Interests.

CURTIS, Smith Curtis, of Rossland, Mine Operator.	◯
SHATFORD, Lytton Wilmot Shatford, of Hedley, Merchant.	X
WINKLER, George Edgar Winkler, of Penticton, Clerk.	◯

Hedley Gazette, 3 January 1907

Trouble On The Similkameen

If ye've got about a minute,
And'll listen while I spin it,
I will tell ye how it went in S'milkameen;
For the Grits imported Curtis
To besmirch us and be-dirt us
An' he done it, too - the best you ever seen.

Now, what hurt us was that Curtis
Aired his linen, while his shirt is
Just as foul as any other demagogue's;
An' he said he'd boost the taxes -
Swore he'd stop the use of axes -
Just by raisin' of the cost of cuttin' logs.

There be some that talk for money -
Some because they think they're funny -
And heaps of them that talk because it's cheap.
But of all the talkin' talkers
There are none that talk like hawkers
Who can beat Smith Curtis on his own dung heap.

There be times, ye know, when Money
Thinks it's not so deuced funny
To be threatened with a pullin' of the leg;
And these men as work for wages
(If they're wise as ancient sages)
Never kill the goose that lays the golden egg.

So we lads, we soon gets leery
Of this animated Query,
And of Dunc who quite forgot his house of glass;
An' we put it up that bellows -
Like these empty-pated fellows -
Ought to get their walkin' papers 'cross the pass.

Then we fellers of this ridin'
Were for thinkin' an' decidin'
That a lobster like Smith Curtis COULDN'T pass;
But that he, like mighty Sampson,
Would be sure to smash the lamps on
Opposition - with the jawbone of an ass.

An' he done it - sure as shootin' –
An' the Grits has quit their hootin'
An' a-slingin' of their mud an' things beside;
But we helped him, though agin' us,
'Cause we couldn't stand McInnis –
Shatford's good enough for us – an' Dick McBride.

Now there's more behind this winnin' –
More that's sinned against than sinnin' -
And the lesson Laurier should ponder well;
For the men of BC, all, sir,
Know the meaning of Cabal, sir,
An' they told those Eastern schemers – "Go to Hades".

Hedley Gazette, 7 February 1907

Mark Your Ballot as Below

SMITH CURTIS *Mining Operator* ROSSLAND	X
L. W. SHATFORD *Merchant* HEDLEY	
GEO. E. WINKLER *Clerk* PENTICTON	

Similkameen Star, 2 February 1907

Armageddon

This poem appeared two days after Thomas Dufferin Pattullo, popularly known as "Duff" Pattullo, leader of the provincial Liberal party, had became BC's premier. It was at the height of the Depression, and Pattullo had been elected on a platform of "Work and Wages", sometimes referred to as "the Little New Deal". The "voucher" in the first stanza of the poem likely refers to the program of food vouchers that were distributed to needy people at the time. Pattullo is referred to as "gazing upon the Yukon" because at the turn of the century he was secretary to the Commissioner of the Yukon.

In stanza two he slays the "C. heifers", i.e. the Conservative Party and also Robert "Doc" Connell, the leader of the Constructivist Party. The defeated Conservatives, led by "Doc Patterson" (Frank Porter Patterson) who surveys his "shattered hopes", won only six seats.

The "Mountain Differential" mentioned in stanza four refers to the differentiated freight rates for different types of goods. Rail carriers charged lower rates for raw materials and basic commodities -- the products of farm, forest, sea, and mine -- than they did for manufactured goods.

The "P.G.E. with figures red" of stanza five was the Pacific Great Eastern Railway (PGE), begun in 1912 and built to connect logging and mining operations in the BC interior with Squamish, where resources could then travel by sea. There were plans to extend the line northwards to Prince George where it would connect with the Grand Trunk Pacific Railway, but during the Depression construction all but ceased. The railway was finally completed to Peace River in 1956. The protracted construction process earned the PGE such nicknames as 'Prince George Eventually", "Past God's Endurance", "Provincial Government Expense". "Please Go Easy" and in the 1950s, "Phil Gaglardi's Express". "Charlie at the throttle" refers to Charles Sidney Leary, who as Minister of Public Works would have been responsible for PGE construction.

The Similkameen riding in the 1937 election included the Similkameen valley as well as the southern Okanagan up to and including Penticton. The riding's winner was Charles Herbert Tupper, the Liberal candidate, who beat Conservative Harry Howes Boyle (mentioned in the penultimate stanza), and Francis Henry (Frank) Brown, the "C. C. F.er" (Cooperative Commonwealth Federation, precursor to the New Democratic Party) mentioned in the sixth stanza (the CCF took the seat in the next election in 1941).

George Matheson Murray, the Liberal candidate for the Lillooet riding immediately north of Similkameen mentioned in stanza seven, did the Highland fling because he was elected. Murray is best known as the husband of Margaret Lally "Ma" Murray, the outspoken editor of the *Bridge River-Lillooet News.* Perley Russell, a prominent Princeton citizen at the time, would have been disappointed because he supported the Conservative party.

Pattullo's plan to "share the wealth" (stanza eight) included a health insurance bill that had been passed in 1936. Implementation was halted, however, over objections from doctors. The reference to "social credit" is perhaps a warning to Pattullo -- the United Farmers of Alberta passed a provincial health insurance bill in 1935 but were defeated by the Social Credit party later that year.

Caddy refers to "Cadborosaurus", Victoria BC's answer to the Loch Ness Monster. First "sighted" in 1933, four years before this verse was published and at the height of the Depression, the Victoria Board of Trade hoped it would do wonders for the local tourist industry, as they thought "Ogopogo", a similar creature, had done for the Okanagan, following its "sighting" in 1926. "Quite by Hoyle", meaning "properly done", refers to Edmond Hoyle, the man who consolidated the rules of whist in the 18th century.

Armageddon

Peerless Pattullo took the stand
With his best Sunday look on,
His KC voucher in his hand,
And gazed upon the Yukon.

His mighty scimitar dripped blood,
His henchmen served him well,
In rows the slain C. heifers stood,
And there lay Doc Connell.

Doc Paterson stood upon the deck,
Surveyed his shattered hopes,
Survivors six clung to the wreck –
They didn't know the ropes.

The Mountain Differential stopped,
Though quite unnecessarily;
Beside the cowcatcher was propped
"On time", if not too early,

The P.G.E. with figures red,
And Charlie at the throttle;
It gave the lie to those who said
Its power came from the bottle.

Now Mr. Brown he came to town,
His pony act was clever,
But Charlie's lariat came down
And holed the CCFer.

Geo. Murray did the Highland fling,
Was Perley disappointed!
And Mr. Black was off he track,
Tom Hooper quite disjointed.

Now "share the wealth" may sound OK
To those who fain would wed it,
But health insurance so they say,
Will be no social credit.

Far called, our navvies melt away,
Forlorn is work and wages,
Although it was, the wise ones say,
The prize of all the ages.

Caddy the swimming worm may know
If it was quite by Hoyle,
That this fair vale of Ogopogo
Should Boyle in Liberal oil.

So we regard with bated breaths
Our images of wax,
And so we die ten thousand deaths
While waiting for the axe.

Similkameen Star, 3 June 1937

Dredging Granite Creek, 1925. Princeton Museum

Thanksgiving Him

This is a fitting poem with which to end. The poem is full of ennui and sums up the author's feelings about the state of the world as seen from Princeton. Published just before Thanksgiving, the poem is a prayer of thanks not to God ("Thou know'st we do not worship thee") but to the "graven gods of currency". Dave Taylor, editor of the *Similkameen Star* at the time, is the author.

The poem begins with the transition from the Depression to the Second World War -- "We sought for butter, we got tanks". The Second World War was ostensibly fought for freedom but Taylor comments that the result was actually "littler Hitlers" and "bureaucracy". The war brought an end to the Depression but Taylor bemoans the fact that rationing was imposed during the war to limit the use of imported food and to free up supplies for the military. Everyone received a ration book, which contained coupons for butter, tea, coffee, and sugar. Ketchup was also rationed because of a shortage of tomatoes. Rationing in Canada ended in 1947.

During the war, markets and labour went through significant upheavals. The "rubber dollar" in line twelve refers to the high inflation rate, which in 1946 was 20%. There was a labour shortage in Canada during the war ("labor playing hide and seek") especially in forestry and agriculture. The interned Japanese-Canadians filled part of this shortage. Taylor says that locally grown food ("pears") was often more expensive than imported food ("grapes"), a situation which still holds true today.

"Last time it was bully beef" refers to the tinned corned beef used during the First World War to feed soldiers, its place taken during the Second World War with "Spam". Spam, which is a precooked, canned pork product, was first developed in 1937 and was widely used during the war. The word is a contraction of "spiced ham". Taylor comments on fashions of the time. Zoot suits, with their high-waisted, wide-legged, tight-cuffed trousers, and long coats with wide lapels were popular during the 1940s, as were juke boxes, and "Revenge of the Zombies" was a 1944 movie in "Technicolor". There appears to have been a shortage of building materials "for houses" – "the only nails are painted red", "we're short of lumber" – "but not for jails".

Taylor comments sardonically on how 'blest" we are to "live in these great times" with the atom bomb (dropped on Hiroshima and Nagasaki in 1945), jet propulsion (first made practicable during the war) and vitamins (vitamin supplements were just beginning to be widely used) even though many are still poor ("Brother, Can You Spare a Dime?" – the title of one of the best-known American songs of the Depression).

"[T]he right to choose between the Arabs and the Jews" refers to the fate of Palestine which was being decided at the time. A month after this poem was published in November 1947, the United Nations voted in favour of the partition of Palestine between Arabs and Jews. Taylor follows this by cheering ironically for the existence of bubble gum (invented in 1928 and popular during the 1940s), swing music (a popular dance music that emerged during the 1930s) and beer. He gives thanks for the "means test" (used to determine eligibility for Old Age Pension), income taxes and the right to vote.

Taylor brings the poem home by referring to the unfinished Hope-Princeton Highway ("More Hope than highway") that was meant to bring prosperity to the region and which was finally finished two years later in October 1949.

Thanksgiving Him, 1947

The time has come to give our thanks;
We sought for butter, we got tanks
We fought for peace and happiness,
We wrought the pieces of a mess.
And smashing Hitler into space
Made littler Hitlers in his place;
And propping up Democracy,
We propped it with bureaucracy.
We won man's right of freedom's rule,
That he be free to play the fool.
They ease our economic collar
With rations and a rubber dollar
And labour playing hide and seek
With shortage and a five day week.
Our markets take fantastic shapes
Our pears out-price imported grapes.
The last time it was bully beef,
Then it was spam, now hard-boiled grief,
Not even humble beans and bacon,
Beloved ketchup quite forsaken.
The only nails are painted red,
The skirts are down, but not the bed;
Zoot suit swing makes juke box duller
Than zombie blues in Technicolor,
And even when you dial the news
It squeaks with rhymes of soleless shoes;
And planes and trains that make the night
Hideous with automaton fright,
And kids, most modern of disasters,
And dogs more ruling than their masters.
In fact this whole inhuman race
Is going fast not any place.
We're short of lumber and of nails
For houses, but we still have jails;
Mistake us not, we're not agin' them,
But just they put the wrong guys in them;
We're short of everything but blether,
They've even Russian-ized our weather;

We've atom bombs and jet propulsion,
And vitamins in Scotch emulsion.
How blest to live in these great times,
But brother, could you spare a dime?
On second thought we hand it back:
They'd have it on our income tax.
Forgive us our hypocrisy,
Thou know'st we do not worship thee
But graven gods of currency.
We thank thee for the right to choose
Between the Arabs and the Jews.
We still can give three rousing cheers
For bubble gum and swing and beers.
And still we have, whate'er our lacks
The means test and the income tax.
We have the right, nay, near compulsion,
To vote our own choice of revulsion.
Our road will bring prosperity,
More Hope than highway though it be.
And though we know our forests' worth
And fill the needs of half the earth
We're lucky that we have enough
Paper to print this worthless stuff.
Ahem.

Similkameen Star, 2 October 1947

Frank William (Billy) Hazzard, undertaker, 1928. Princeton Museum

Chapter 14: Earning a Living

Many of the verses that appear in this collection are about work and most of them are distributed throughout the other chapters of this book. This chapter is therefore a pot pourri of disparate verses about work not included in other chapters. They are arranged chronologically and cover a wide range of jobs.

People spend a large proportion of their lives earning a living – most people work for about forty years, that is, about two-thirds of their adult lives. It is interesting to reflect, then, on how little of the literature we read, the films we see and the music we listen to are about work. It is as though we use culture to escape from work rather than as a means to come to terms with it.

The work poems in this collection provide an interesting picture of the changing nature of work and attitudes towards it in the upper Similkameen during the early years of the 20th century. The prospector who on the one hand speaks of being a "King in a vast demesne" and not a "cog in a vast machine" but then goes on to complain about the snow; the miner who praises his beloved candlestick; the "gallant" nurse who battles the flu in the hospital - all these characters provide snapshots of attitudes towards work prevalent at the time.

The Thinker praises the brain behind the brawn of each job – the "clear-eyed man who knows," the "mind which plans them". The poem was written by Berton Braley (1882-1966), an American poet who published many poetry books throughout his life including *Songs of a Mining Camp* (1909) about his experiences in Butte, Montana. Braley was known as the "bard of individualism and capitalism", a label that is certainly demonstrated in this poem, which is not so much about the worker than about the boss ("the eye which scans them") and the investor who is "making the dream come true".

The Thinker

Back of the beating hammer
By which the steel is wrought,
Back of the workshop's clamour,
The seeker may find the Thought,
The Thought that is ever master
Of iron and steam and steel,
That rises above disaster
And tramples it under heel!

The drudge may fret and tinker
Or labour with dusty blows,
But back of him stands the Thinker,
The clear-eyed man who Knows;
For into each plow or sabre,
Each piece and part and whole,
Must go the Brains of Labor
Which gives the work a soul!

Back of the motor's humming,
Back of the belts that sing,
Back of the hammer's drumming,
Back of the cranes that swing,
There is the eye which scans them,
Watching through stress and strain,
There is the Mind which plans them -
Back of the brawn, the Brain!

Might of the roaring boiler,
Force of the engine's thrust,
Strength of the sweating toiler,
Greatly in these we trust,
But back of them stands the Schemer,
The Thinker who drives things through,
Back of the job - the Dreamer
Who's making the dream come true!

Similkameen Star, 24 October 1913

The Workers' Song

Originally called "Fifty Thousand Lumberjacks", this song concerns a state-wide loggers' strike in Washington in 1917 that changed the identity of the logger from an outcast, blanket-toting timberbeast into a highly respected worker welcomed anywhere. No other strike in history has so transformed lifestyles. The loggers were members of the Industrial Workers of the World, known as the IWW or "Wobblies" or "Wobs" and the song first appeared in *IWW Songs to Fan the Flames of Discontent*, otherwise known as the *Little Red Songbook*, in September 1917. The song's appearance in the *Similkameen Star* two years later occurred at a time of massive labour unrest throughout North America, including the Winnipeg General strike of spring 1919.

The summer of 1919 also saw two major protracted strikes in the Similkameen, one by railway workers and one by recently unionized loggers. In January 1919, the BC Loggers' Union was formed and over the course of that year it signed up 15,000 members throughout the province. In July, it joined the One Big Union (OBU), a coalition of the IWW, socialists and trade unionists that was interested in establishing direct workers' control over economic and political life, and changed its name to the Lumber Workers Industrial Union (LWIU). By 1920, seventy percent of the province's logging work force belonged to the union.

By June of 1919, the railway workers were back on the job but the loggers were still on strike. On 27 June 1919, two months before this song was published in the *Similkameen Star* the union publicized its revised demands in the form a letter to the editor.

1. Nine hours per day and a minimum wage of 45 cents per hour for common labour
2. That six days constitute a week's work and all overtime must be paid for by time-and-a-half.
3. Axe men and drill men, $4.50 per day, nine hours.
4. Four horse teamsters, $125 and board. Two horse

teamsters, $100 and board. Single horse teamsters to be paid 45 cents per hour.

5. Cooks $150 per month and board. Second cooks, $90; flunkies, $70; bullocks, $75.
6. Blacksmiths 55 cents per hour. Blacksmith's helpers, 45 cents per hour.
7. Board to be at the rate of $1.15 per day.
8. That all station men who are in town and want to go back

on their jobs to be paid at the rate of 50 cents per hour for all work already done.

9. That we have the right to choose our own doctor.
10. There shall be no discrimination against any of the men who are on strike.

(Signed) STRIKE COMMITTEE Per: H. Allman

Was the editor in accord with the loggers' demands? The fact that he published them in full suggests that he might have been sympathetic, and yet two months earlier he wrote: "bolshevism…does not recognize the employer, government, law, order or private property. The employer and employee are allies. The Bolshevik is their common enemy." The position of a small town newspaper editor is fraught with contradictions.

"The Workers' Song" was published in the *Similkameen Star* without any comment. We do not know who Frank Floranse was, but suspect he was a local logger who had a copy of the *Little Red Songbook*, and that he copied and submitted the song to the *Similkameen Star* for publication during the loggers' strike. However, the song was recopied and published with two lines (the first two lines of stanza 2) missing and a typo ("Fifty" for "Fatty"). The complete version below is from the 1934 edition of the *Little Red Songbook*.

Logging camp near Hedley

The Workers' Song

Fifty thousand lumberjacks, fifty thousand packs,
Fifty thousand dirty rolls of blankets on their backs;
Fifty thousand minds made up, strike and strike like men,
For fifty years they have packed a bed, but never will again.

Chorus
Such a lot of devils, that's what the papers say;
They've gone on strike for shorter hours, and some increase in pay;
They left the camps, the lazy tramps, they all walked out as one;
They say they'll win the strike or put the bosses on the bum.

Fifty thousand wooden bunks full of things that crawl;
Fifty thousand restless men have left them once for all.
One by one they dared not say, "Fat, the hours are long!";
If they did they'd hike -- but now they're fifty thousand strong.

Fatty rich, we know your game; know your pride is pricked:
Say, why not be a man and know when you are licked.
They've joined the One Big Union - gee - for goodness' sake get wise,
The more you try to buck them now, the more they organize.

Take a tip; start right in, plan some cozy rooms,
Six or eight spring beds in each, with towels, sheets and brooms;
Shower baths for men who work keeps them well and fit;
A laundry, too, and drying room would help a little bit.

Get some dishes, white and clean, good pure food to eat;
See that cook has help enough to keep the table neat.
Tap the bell for eight hours work, treat the boys like men,
And fifty thousand lumberjacks may come to work again.

Men who work should be well paid – "A man's a man for a' that."
Many a man has a home to keep, same as yourself, Old Fat;
Mothers, sisters, sweethearts, wives, children too, galore,
Stand behind the men to win this bread and butter war.

Similkameen Star, 29 August 1919

The Guy at the Crank

This verse is about the projectionist who toils away in his box high up in the rear of the movie theatre. For the entire length of a feature film, he is sentenced to this tiny box, surrounded by the noise of the projector and the heat generated by the electric motor and the bulb. In order to project light the length of the theatre to the screen, the bulb must be very strong. It generates considerable heat, which in the narrow confines of the projectionist's box must at times have been overwhelming. The poem likens the job to a prison sentence and suggests that if the projectionist goes to hell, the devil will exhort him in the midst of the flames to "twist that crank".

The expression, "twist that crank" hearkens back to the early days of film when films were short and projectors were cranked by hand. By the time this verse appeared in the *Princeton Star* in 1920, long feature films were the norm and projectors were run by electric motors. Feature-length movies began being produced in the 1910s, but the first feature-length movie to be advertised in the *Similkameen Star* was D.W. Griffith's "The Love Flower" on 14 October 1921.

Although the *Star* suggests that C. Bridges of Cranbrook wrote the poem, it was in fact written by Ernest Eade and was published in several American newspapers in 1914. The poem likely found its way into the *Star* via the editor who saw it in the Cranbrook newspaper to whom C. Bridges had sent it.

Princeton in 1895. Princeton Museum

The Guy at the Crank

Did you ever go to a picture show,
And sit in the dark and stare,
And wonder how in creation
The picture got there?
It isn't the soft, slick manager
Whom you have to thank;
It's the half-baked, oily son of a gun
Who cusses and twists the crank.

He goes to his little two-by-four,
Iron-walled like a prison cell;
He starts to make the film chase thru
And soon it's hotter than - well.
You talk of the steamship stoker,
And the heat of his fire's bank
But a stoker's dream is like ice cream
To the chap that turns the crank.

To the picture show is where you go
To sit in the dark and stare.
You forget there's another world outside,
When you're snugly seated there:
You watch the actors play their parts,
To you it's all a dream;
But it's very real to the guy at the wheel
Of the picture show machine.

Just where do operators go
When they leave this vale of tears?
Is there some cold place in celestial space
Where they pass their after years?
Or do they mingle with the strong,
Where sulphurous fumes are rank
And hear old Nick when the flames are thick
Shout, "Hey, there, twist that crank"?

Princeton Star, 16 April 1920

WOMEN'S WORK

"She Has No Occupation", "Starvation Wages", and "A Mother's Prayer"

Historically, much of the work done by women has been unrecognized and the work poems from the upper Similkameen reflect this invisibility. One reason for this is that in the days of early settlement, men vastly outnumbered women. In 1901, for example, there were 256 men in Princeton but only sixty women. It was men who set up the ranches, did the prospecting, built the railways and worked in the mines – most railway workers and miners were either single or had left families behind to come and work. It was also men who published the newspapers. It's no wonder, then, that women's experiences are not reflected in the verses published there. The next three items are an exception.

She Has No Occupation

A majority of the verses published in the newspapers were published anonymously, so it is impossible to tell whether the authors were men or women. This first poem does, however, name a woman author who celebrates women's work, while at the same time recognizing its invisibility. Elsie Duncan Yale, its author, was an American poet popular in the first few decades of the 20th century. She also composed hymns under the pseudonym "Gracie Gordon".

Princeton Museum

She Has No Occupation

She rises up at break of day,
And through her tasks she races;
She cooks the meal as best she may,
And scrubs the children's faces.
While schoolbooks, lunches, ribbons, too,
All need consideration,
And yet the census man insists
She has 'no occupation'.

When breakfast dishes all are done,
She bakes a pudding, maybe;
She cleans the rooms up one by one,
With one eye watching baby;
The mending pile she then attacks,
By way of variation,
And yet the census man insists
She has 'no occupation'.

She irons for a little while,
Then presses pants for daddy;
She welcomes with a cheery smile
Returning lass and laddie.
A hearty dinner next she cooks
(No time for relaxation),
And yet the census man insists
She has 'no occupation'.

For lessons that the children learn
The evening scarce is ample -
To mother dear they always turn
For help with each example.
In grammar and geography
She finds her relaxation,
And yet the census man insists
She has 'no occupation'.

Princeton Star, 26 March 1920

Starvation Wages

This piece about working in a laundry was published in the *Similkameen Star* on 19 October 1923. Although it is not a poem or a song, it is included here because it describes the kind of dreary jobs that were available to women in the early years of the 20th century:

> Vancouver, Oct. 15. "Can a working girl keep herself respectable, live in comfort and have an opportunity of self betterment at the night schools while working in a laundry at $10 a week?" Following a stirring and sensational exposé in *The Hook*, published by J. S. Cowper, ex-M. P., a public outcry has been directed toward conditions that are about to be presented to the government for immediate remedial action. The women's clubs are taking the matter up, and a probe is being started. This movement was precipitated by Miss Greta P. Fraser, a bright and respectable girl of 21 who told of the arduous toil of laundry girls; and, in citing her own case, it seems that she was "fired" because she asked for enough money to live in decency. Miss Fraser stated to *The Hook* that hers was but one instance. She wished to better herself and attend night school; but was too wearied with back-breaking, monotonous toil to even eat her supper after the day's work, but frequently fell into an exhausted sleep; without undressing after returning to her room.

A Mother's Prayer

This poem is more commonly known as "The Kitchen Prayer" or, among Catholics, "The Kitchen Catechism", and has been hung on many a kitchen wall to inspire the resident housewife in her labours. Its Christian sentiments are based on 1 Corinthians 10:31: "Whether, then, you eat or drink or whatever you do, do all to the glory of God". Its publication in the *Similkameen Star* in 1944 is in keeping with the notion of women doing their share on the home front while the men are fighting overseas. The poem's author is not given, but research attributes it to Cecily Hallack, a minor Catholic novelist and poet. One account suggests that it was made in 1928 by a nineteen-year-old domestic servant in England; another, that it was originally written to console a violinist who was spoiling her hands with kitchen work during the Great War. The claim that it was made by a servant does, however, shed an entirely different light on the poem. If the sentiments are those of a servant, then her prayer is not that of a mother celebrating her service to family and God but rather that of a toiling worker trying to lighten the load of her drudgery. It is interesting to speculate, however, how the poem found its way into the pages of the *Similkameen Star*. Perhaps it was hanging on a kitchen wall in Princeton and was forwarded to the editor to inspire the women on the home front five years into Second World War.

Manning Park, 1943. The Allan Gill Collection

A Mother's Prayer

Lord of all pots and pans and things, since I've no time to be
A saint by doing lovely things, or watching late with Thee;
Or dreaming in the dawnlight, or storming Heaven's Gates,
Make me a saint by getting meals and washing up the plates.

Although I must have Martha's hands I have a Mary's mind,
And when I black the boots and shoes, Thy sandals, Lord, I find.
I think of how they trod the earth, what time I scrub the floor;
Accept this meditation, Lord, I haven't time for more.

Warm all the kitchen with Thy love, and light it with Thy peace,
Forgive me all my worrying and make all grumbling cease;
Thou who didst love to give men food, in room, or by the sea.
Accept this service that I do - I do it unto Thee.
Similkameen Star, 11 May 1944

Chapter 15: The Natural World

The high mountains and forests of the Similkameen valley were a very different environment from what the settlers knew "back home", but their attitude towards nature had been formed by the world they had left behind.

Many of the early Similkameen settlers were from urban Britain. The massive industrialization of Britain during the latter half of the 19th century meant that more and more people moved into the cities. Their only experience of the natural world would likely have been walking among the fields and hedgerows of the countryside surrounding the cities. Their view of nature might have been influenced by the Romantic poets of the 18th and 19th centuries who viewed it in a spiritual, even pantheistic way. Imagine the settlers' shock upon first encountering the wilds of the Similkameen valley! Susan Allison, one of the Similkameen valley's earliest settlers, expresses her reaction with these lines:

> Environed by stern mountains, now I felt
> Pent in hell's darkest, deepest prison walls

The rapid advances in science during the 19th century began to demystify nature and to transform the Romantics' pantheism into a view of nature as God's creation. In 1911, a reader of the *Similkameen Star*, for example, in his/her poem **Evening** embraces the twilight when workers can go home and rest and "Night steals on apace/For so God wills". Susan Allison, under her *nom de plume* Stratton Moir shares this divine view of nature in her 1914 poem **Omnipresence**. A year later **The Spring Flight** speaks of the wilderness as the earth as it was "left by God." The Romantic, pantheistic view of nature did not, however, entirely disappear. Dave Taylor, editor of the *Similkameen Star*, in his poem **Lyra**, personifies aspects of nature with names from Greek mythology.

For settlers from the relatively benign climate of Britain, the weather in the Similkameen valley must have been hard to bear.

In their new surroundings, some poets wrote in the vernacular, as evidenced in four poems about spring – **Spring, When the Snow is Falling, A Springlet** and **Oh, the Snow Went Away But It Came Back Again. Fly Time** expresses a further complaint about life in the valley. **Spring in Similkameen**, however, celebrates the turning of the season from winter to summer, with vivid descriptions of the natural and human transformations taking place. The poem is most probably by Dave Taylor, editor of the *Star* at the time, but lacks the mythological references of his pseudo-romantic "Lyra" of twelve years earlier. **Spring Poetry** comments on the "spring poet" who composes such verse and accuses him of snorting and braying "like a demented ass." The mention of "Muttering Jimmy" in Taylor's poem refers to a Princeton character called "Singing Jimmy" who was reputed to have been a vaudeville ventriloquist and who used to startle adults and delight children by making lampposts "talk".

With settlements built in the midst of forests, fire was a constant danger. **He Lit a Match** talks about how carelessness can start a forest fire. **The Fire Demon** is about a fire that nearly engulfed Coalmont and Blakeburn.

The poems mentioned so far have all been very public, expressing points of view that were likely shared by many. **Little Ducks on Turtle Lake** is a very personal poem about enjoying local nature. It recounts the experiences of two friends lying in their tent listening to the sounds of the night -- coyotes, owls, far-off trains -- and watching the ducks congregating in the middle of Turtle Lake. The poem's author is unknown but it is dedicated to H.D. Barnes, a Hedley historian.

Nature poetry was a well-known genre in the early years of the last century and Similkameen newspapers contained many such poems with titles such as "Beautiful Snowflake", "Blossoms" and "The Infinite". The practicalities and difficulties of life in the Similkameen, however, also gave rise to some very down-to-earth poems about the qualities of nature in the upper Similkameen.

Omnipresence

I sat upon the sea beach
To hear the sad sea sing,
Screaming gulls flew o'er me
With scarcely moving wing.

The waves were breaking softly
Upon the silver sand;
The dull grey sky was lowering,
A storm was hard at hand:

The waves took on the colour
Of the grey lowering sky,
The waves began to whisper
Of men about to die.

But still I sat and listened -
The winds began to blow,
And lashed the waves to fury,
Their crests gleamed white as snow.

A madness seemed to seize them -
They rushed across the sand,
With wild tremulous laughter
As if to engulf the land.

Then sweeping swiftly backward,
With frenzied rush they tore
The wreckage that was scattered
From off the sandy shore.

As rapidly returning,
Rearing in seething foam,
Threw back the broken fragments
With sob and hollow groan.

Dark purple clouds came creeping
Over the dull grey sky,
And stained the dull grey ocean
With a dark and purple dye.

And as I sat serenely,
Beside the seething sea,
A Voice came from the waters
And whispered thus to me:

"I am the changing ocean;
I am the changing sky;
I am the winds that murmur,
I am the gulls that fly.

"I am all life - life and motion;
I am all strength and power;
Seek where you will find me,
In a star, or in a flower.

"Always changing, I change not,
I am ever the same;
Although my aspects vary
The Absolute, my name.

"Fear not the raging waters
Fear not the changing skies -
Know all, that life is immortal
Know that it cannot die.

"Fear not the sins of mortals
Fear not the errors they make,
The cause of disease and disaster
For our dead Master's sake."

Similkameen Star, 13 March 1914

The Spring Flight

It's northward, ever northward, where no man's foot has trod,
Where clean air sweeps the tundras and earth is near to God;
Where blue waves are a-tossing, the long still night is o'er,
Where giant bergs are heaving and spring has waked once more;
They come and pass and still obey the summons loud and long,
The laggards and the weaklings fail, the race is to the strong;
The great blue heron beats his way, the eagle seeks the pines,
And high o'erhead are pelicans and cranes in waving lines;
With whistling wings, black duck and teal in scouting bands dash by,
The avocet in mottled garb, wild swans with changing cry;
The curlew's call, the killdeer's note, are heard by day and night,
The mallard's surging rush of wing, the redshank's flickering flight;
Untired the mighty hosts still pass o'er Yukon's lonely mines,
The honking geese in endless ranks, great gulls in long low lines;
The watchful peregrine takes toll, the wheeling kite's full-fed,
The eagles', owls' and falcons' claws with bloody stain are red;
But crested grebe and laughing loon are on the heaving swell,
And in that far, far northland, a myriad voices tell
The joy of life worth living, where no man's foot has trod,
Where clean air sweeps the nesting grounds and earth's as left by God.

Hedley Gazette, 13 May 1915

Lyra

'Tis evening, and on planished wings
Soft footed Iris dips her vial
Into the oily green of dusk,
As dims the shadow on the dial.

And in the embers of the day
She fires her torch and flings aloft
Its flame and floods the graying orb
With rosy-fingered vapours, soft.

Silken ochres, mystic mauves
And milky browns. The agate bowl
Hovers between the dusk and dark,
Trembles like a departing soul.

And Charon poles his dismal course,
The while Eolus sighs a dirge,
And far upon the eastern rim
The harbingers of night emerge.

So Iris with her wand alight,
As Hera puts the day to flight,
Trips o'er the heavens in delight,
Lighting the tapers of the night.

A single steely point of blue,
A single steely strident tone;
Vega appears high in the east
And for a moment rules alone.

But joining hands about her soon,
Each in a pinken pantaloon,
Her sisters five wink at the moon,
And dance and trill an airy tune.

And Orpheus takes the magic lyre
And plucks the strings of silvered light,
And bends the haughty mountain tops
And works the witchery of night.

In olden times the Argonauts
A refuge found in Lyra's skill
More potent than the sirens' wiles
Or e'en the stout Ulysses' will.

Similkameen Star, 16 June 1938

Spring

The leaves refuse to bud upon the trees
While Winter's chilly breath is in the air:
O hurry Spring and break his heavy bonds,
And drive him northward to his icy lair.

With smiling face chase Winter's storms away,
And let the rivers all run glad and free;
Bring from the south our friends the happy birds
And bid them call from every shrub and tree.

Too long the dreary snow has covered o'er
Your pleasant handiwork of former times,
So hasten Spring and quickly raise the siege -
For I am running awful short of rhymes.

Similkameen Star, 14 March 1903

When the Snow Is Falling

When the snow is falling, how beautiful it looks,
A-clinging on the bushes an' whirling in the nooks;
But when the rain is falling, it goes of with a rush;
'Tis then the picture vanishes: there's no sentiment in slush.

Similkameen Star, 26 January 1901

A Springlet

From off the running rivulet the icy chain is thawed,
And the quacklet of the ducklet in the land is heard abroad,
And the songlet of the birdlet re-echoes through the air,
And the bawlet of the bullet is heard in meadows fair,
And the croaklet of the froglet makes the evening shadows zing,
All of which moves us to mention, gentle reader, this is Spring.

Similkameen Star, 1 April 1908

Oh, The Snow Went Away But It Came Back Again

When you get over the shoe heads in mud and you feel like saying something, just hum over this ditty to the tune of "Turkey in the Straw", you will find it very soothing:

Oh, the snow went away but it came back again,
Off again and on again like Finnegan's train,
But the mud sticks around like the fleas on a mutt -
This sort o' sticky stuff we have nothing else but.

Princeton Star, 8 April 1926

Fly Time

Busy, thirsty, noxious fly,
We're at war, sir, you and I!
Once the poet let you sup
Freely from his brimming cup:
Now we know you carry germs –
Nevermore can we make terms!
Leave, I warn you, my domain
For I'm planning a campaign!
Sticky paper's out of date;
Screens too oft you penetrate.
But I'll summon to my aid
Weapons that you can't evade.
I will spread a poisoned bait
That shall lure you to your fate.
Subtle fumes of formalin
Shall destroy you and your kin!
I will catch you in a net,
Cunning traps of wire I'll set.
Germicides I'll spray around:
Not a corner shall be found
Where a hungry fly can feed,
Not a nook where you can breed.
Filthy, germ-infested fly,
Warning fair I give hereby –
We're at war, sir, you and I!

Coalmont Courier, 5 August 1912

Similkameen Star
4 August 1949

Spring in Similkameen

It's springtime in the hills again,
With wispy winds and wistful rain,
And hope's rebirth in pleasant pain,
In secret stir and cheerful strain:
Th'eternal ode of wax and wane,
A new round and an old refrain.

Where seasons linger, loath to go,
But mellower in their ripeness so -
On this stern stage of sun and snow
Deft interludes of afterglow.

The thin moon soothes the field of night
And flails a staff of star delight;
The round noon sits on higher throne
And wins the hill world for his own.

High up the slopes of Hozomeen,
The white is pierced by spears of green
By little lakes that grow from snows
Beside the snow th'anemone blows.

The churlish hills, still pocked with snow,
Are loath to let their languor go.
But storming greens in swift surprise
To scale the rocky ramparts rise.

The strong sun sails, aye prowing fore;
Where waves of cloud break from the shore
And deep down on the valley's floor
The river rumbles to a rising roar.

In fitful clouds the vexed hours fly,
In truant sun and fretful sky,
Whereout in passing pageant spills
The evolution of our hills.

The canopy of virgin snows
Is tarnished as the young year grows;
Emerges slow the bald cocoon,
Fuzzed with an infant green full soon.

Till yellow daisies stamp their sway
And rule a brief but brilliant day;
Then verdure rises rich to reign,
Till summer sears the brow again;
In dwindling days the passing show
Is claimed again by ancient snow.

In pageantry of sound and smell
The magic wand taps dune and dell,
With catkins purring in the brakes
And sleek trout sportive in the lake.

The phallic ooze of heaving earth,
The sweet smoke of the woodsman's hearth,
E'en the old church bell's throb is musked
In length'ning overtones of dusk.

With wisps of wind and raps of rain,
Sweet evidence of chang'ling pain,
One with the seed its kiss unchains,
The season's budding in the grain.

And in the medley of the hours
A panoply of vanguard flowers,
Where pansies pout and tulips spill,
Tumbling on snowdrop, daffodil.

The robin's ripe complacent air,
The naiad bluebird's furtive lair,
The saucy sparrow's mocking gawk,
And high aloft the scouring hawk.

And here in nature's breed of men
The spade and hammer sprout again,
The young man's fancy, says the verse,
Doth run to better or to worse.

Voici la mode Parisienne;
And Bronc's shirts worn outside again.
Out comes Virginny's string and twig
And Mutterin' Jimmy's sprightly jig.

And Gilbert toils among his tulips
And mops his brow and thinks of juleps;
The Cenotaph, reviving leper,
Is sprinkled rich with Martin's Pepper.

The roads rub out their icy rust
In pools of water and of dust,
And skis and sleds abandon hopes
To marbles, balls and skipping ropes.

The first stiff fly in fuming fuss,
The first frail moth, sad-humorous;
Silvester's frog booms baritone,
That summer's come and winter's gone;

And swift will surge the rushing green,
Pine-tinctured air and sky serene,
And swaying bunchgrass' silken sheen
And summer in Similkameen.

Similkameen Star, 10 May 1950

Singing Jimmy. Princeton Museum

Spring Poetry

This is the season of mud and slush,
When the spring poet begins to gush
Of budding trees and sprouting grass -
He snorts and brays like a demented ass.

Similkameen Star, 27 March 1912

He Lit A Match

He struck a match as he passed through
The glorious growth of centuries;
He lit his pipe - and then he threw
The tiny blaze among the trees.
It flickered, seemed to die away -
And he, all careless, passed along,
Filled with the pleasure of the day,
The glory of the forest's song.

Furious, wild-driven by the gale
That roared as hell is thought to roar,
The forest fire swept hill and vale,
Claiming its victims by the score.
Huge flame-tongues covered every place
That even seemed to offer hope,
And devastation smote earth's face;
No power save God's with this could cope.

Black are the hills where stood the trees
That graced them so short time ago;
No more their green boughs to the breeze
Swing gently, waving to and fro;
Black are the stumps and dry the rills
That yesterday so joyous went;
But blackest is it that these ills
Are suffered by the innocent.

Hedley Gazette, 18 June 1914

GUARD AGAINST FIRE.

One of a series of "Prevent Forest Fires" ads in the *Princeton Star* in 1919. This one appeared on 1 August.

The Fire Demon

Recently every available citizen in Blakeburn and Coalmont was pressed into service by the district fire warden to assist in combating the forest fire that threatened at the time to destroy both of our neighbouring coal camps. Including among these willing workers was our Blakeburn Correspondent, "Jay Ell" who has very deftly put his experience in verse, and in the concluding stanza pointed a moral which will carry its own appeal.

A wreath of smoke that barely could be seen,
Far floating upward from the forest dense,
Had caught the ranger's eye, alertly keen,
And brought him to a halt - expectant, tense.

E'en as he gazed the smoke cloud grew apace,
And thickening waves were wafted by the wind;
Till fiercely wind-fanned flames rose up to race
From tree to tree while fiery uproar dinned.
With speed the ranger reached the nearest phone

To broadcast forth the news, that message dire -
That help was wanted in the woodland zone
To fight the menace of a forest fire.

Then gathered men from north, south, east and west,
A motley crew from mine and mill and store,
Imbued with one desire to do their best
To save the forest from the fire's furore.

Hour after hour, with vim and needful rush,
They hewed a breach with cross-cut saw and axe;
A half-mile line where tangled underbrush
And criss-cross windfalls gave them no relax.

And ever nearer drew the demon blaze;
Thick clouds of smoke came drifting on amain,
It caught their throats and eyes, till in a daze,
They coughed and cursed, then carried on again.
And so for days the weary fight went on;

BE CAREFUL.

Another "Prevent Forest Fires" ad. *Princeton Star* 25 July 1919

The while the fierce inferno came ahead,
And timbers which a hundred years had grown,
Crashed to the ground charred, mangled, useless, dead.

And on the fateful day the fire was foiled,
There loomed before the eyes a saddening scene;
A leafless, treeless waste; a heritage despoiled;
A fire charred ruin where the woods had been.

Only an ember from a campfire left,
A fool-flung match or stub of cigarette.
Our forest ravished; citizens, bereft;
And then an aftermath of vain regret.

Princeton Star, 12 August 1926

Little Ducks On Turtle Lake

The little ducks on Turtle Lake,
When light of day was nearly spent,
Would to the centre all betake,
As we observed them from our tent.

Our camp, within a black-pine grove,
Faced out upon the water bright,
And we could watch for any move
They made upon a moon-lit night.

Coyotes howled, the owls would hoot,
The mule deer browsed along the shore,
A far-off train would snort and toot
And climbing grades would puff and roar.

But always, till the break of day,
The little ducks on Turtle Lake
Close-huddled in a flock would stay,
And then at dawn were all awake.

Similkameen Star, 28 January 1943

Chapter 16: Just for Fun

Producing a weekly paper, with the endless need for entertaining copy, must be a strain and a chore at times. Much material travelled between newspapers to be used as fill when some promised article failed to turn up. Oftentimes it was called "Exchange", and our first piece here, **Feller Called Exchange,** is itself an exchange piece, having been picked up from the *Baltimore American.*

Much of this exchange material was light verse, exemplified by the next four pieces. The BC source for **Men and Monkeys** was the *CCF News.* Today it can be found across the Internet, but never with an author or a date attached to it. **Epitaphs** was claimed to be the work of Frank Smith of Buffalo, but the earliest we can find it in print is in New Zealand's *Poverty Bay Herald* in June 1908, a month before it appeared in Princeton. Those readers who remember taking Latin in school (a declining number, surely) will appreciate **A Latin Romance**, a set of verses that has appeared in numerous school magazines. It arrived in Princeton in December 1913, but had been in print since at least 1889. **Served Him Right** similarly had travelled before seeing print here in Coalmont in 1912.

Next come two local pieces. The first, **The Eagle is a Noble Bird**, is from 1904 and the second, **Sandy McSterrit**, is from the pen of Jay Ell, poet laureate of Tulameen.

We can say little about our last three verses, **Paul Dehn's Typist is Off On Holiday, A Bit of Treatment,** and **Can You?**; research brings up nothing for any of them. We can say that Paul Dehn was a British screenwriter, and that **Can You?** is a fine parody of Rudyard Kipling's well-known poem "If".

Feller Called Exchange

I read that all the funny stuff these humorous fellers writes,
And laughin' at their foolishness is one of my delights.
Sometimes they're sure too deep for me and I can't catch th' nub,
But I laugh at 'em anyway t'show I ain't no scrub.
But of 'em all for writin' stuff, that's funny, quaint and strange,
The best is that there chap that signs his jokes an' things "Exchange."

When I go hikin' down th' page a-reading all th' fun
I always find a lot of his - a dozen if there's one.
An' seems t'me there's none the rest gets quite the sort o' twist
This feller likes to give things; so in making out the list
O' things to make 'em holler when it's my night at the grange
I memerize a lot o' things writ by that man "Exchange."

Er mebby he's a woman, 'cause he's talking all th' time
A-gittin' off some foolishness or reelin' off some rhyme.
I'd like to know what paper he's a-writin' steady fer,
An' I'd subscribe an' get his jokes as fast as they occur.
An' t'other day I read a piece, "To Cure a Dog of Mange,"
An' when I reached the end I found 'twas writ by that "Exchange."

He must be 'bout th' biggest chap they is; he's 'bout a mile
Ahead of this hyer Kiplin' that they say's so versatyle;
They ain't no subject goin' that this feller can't set down
An' tell you all about it, fer he's got th' facts down brown.
Th' more I study on it w'y th' more th' thing seems strange
That any feller knows as much as that man called "Exchange."

Similkameen Star, 30 June 1903

Men And Monkeys

Three monkeys sat in a coconut tree,
Discussing things as they're said to be.
Said one to the others, "Now listen, you two,
There's a certain rumour that can't be true;
That man descended from our noble race!
The very idea is a disgrace!
No monkey ever deserted his wife
Starved her babies and ruined her life,
And you've never known a mother monkey
To leave her babies with others to bunk;
Or to pass them on from one to another
Till they scarcely know who is their mother.
And another thing you'll never see -
A monkey build a fence 'round a coconut tree
And let the coconuts go to waste,
Forbidding all other monkeys a taste.
Why, if I'd put a fence 'round the tree,
Starvation would force you to steal from me!
Here's another thing a monkey won't do -
Go out at night and get on a stew,
Or use a gun or club or knife
To take some other monkey's life.
Yes, man descended, the ornery cuss,
But brother, he didn't descend from us!"

Similkameen Star, 30 March 1944

Tunnel #1 on the Kettle Valley Railway just west of Princeton. Princeton Museum

Epitaphs

[As they might have been written]

Here lies a man who seemed to think
His troubles he could drown in drink.
(He succeeded.)

Here lies a chap quite free from strife,
Who dared to contradict his wife.
(She's married again.)

A hypnotist below doth lie
Who looked a tiger in the eye.
(And the tiger won.)

Dear friends, here lie the bones of one
Who always carried a deadly gun.
(The other man drew first.)

Below a man quite safely lies,
Who jumped a chap just twice is size.
(Take warning.)

Kind friends, stop here and please take note -
Here lies the fellow who rocked the boat.
(Companions were rescued.)

Similkameen Star, 15 July 1908

A Latin Romance

Boyibus kissibus sweetum girlorum,
Girlibus likibus, wantum summorum,
Pater puellibus enter parlorum,
Kickibus boyibus exibus dorum,
Nightibus darkibus, homum limporum,
Climibus fencibus, breechibus torum.

Similkameen Star, 5 December 1913

Served Him Right

He criticized her puddings and found fault with her cake,
He wished she'd make such biscuits as his mother used to make.
She didn't wash the dishes, and she didn't make a stew
Nor even mend his stockings, as his mother used to do.
His mother had six children, but by night her work was done -
His wife was always drudging, and yet had only one.
His mother always was well dressed - his wife could be so, too,
If she would only manage, as his mother used to do.
Ah, well, she wasn't perfect, but she tried to do her best,
Until at length she thought her time had come to take a rest;
And so one day when he the same old harangue went through,
She turned and boxed his ears, as his mother used to do.

Coalmont Courier, 28 October 1912

The Eagle Is A Noble Bird

The eagle is a noble bird
And wings its flight on high.
The grouse is of lowlier mould
But makes a better fry.

Similkameen Star, 13 August 1904

Sandy MacSterrit

"Oh, hoot mon", said Sandy MacSterrit,
"Ah think that there's nae place like Merritt;
Of course it is true that mah wife's there th' noo,
And maybe that's why ah prefer it."

Similkameen Star, 26 October 1923

Paul Dehn's Typist Is Off on Holiday

My typist is gone on hir holiday
My typist has gohn on a spree
Mx typish hap gone oh hyr haliduy
O gring bacq m! hypist to me.
Bling bac? oK £ring back
Oh bynK b4ck my tipisth to mi tu mo.
Brung bicq ocsling 8acK
Oh blynK ba“K mg t$pys? tp m!. O demn –

The Similkameen Star, 8 August 1945

A Bit of Treatment

When at eve I sit beside her
And caress her soft black hair,
I am blessed with sweet contentment.
Life is calm and peaceful there.

When the daily strife is ended
And, a-weary of the fight,
I direct my footsteps homeward,
Glad for rest that comes with night.

At the gate she always meets me -
Greets me in her cheery way,
And I quite forget the harsh words
That I had in mind to say.

Always patient, kind and faithful,
Helpful, constant, true: I vow
She is worthy, and I love her.
(She's a splendid Holstein cow).

Similkameen Star, 1 December 1916

Can You?

Whether it is owing to the unusual weather conditions, or to some other cause, or that it just happened so, we are not in a position to state, but certain it is that during the past week an unusually large number of people both from Princeton and near-by places have been suffering with acute trouble from their teeth. Faces, distorted by swelling from abscesses and suffering, have been quite common and the dentist has been kept unusually busy. To those who have never had occasion to patronize a dentist the following lines may be lacking in appeal but to them only:

If you can keep your nerve when all about you
I'm placing instruments you hate to see;
If you can grip yourself when I'm about to
Bear down upon a nerve not tenderly;
If you can grin, and not bite when I'm grinding,
Or when you hear me snarl, don't try to speak
Because my office-girl I'm merely asking
To get another drill before next week:

If you can dream, but not of what I'm doing;
If you can think, and hold your thoughts in check;
If you can take a probe, or a clean scraping
And keep your luncheon down below your neck;
If you can bear to hear the burr's swift whirring,
As up and down a nerve I softly play,
And hold yourself without a muscle stirring,
And then come back for more again next day;

If you can let me grab the tooth that's aching;
Grasp tight the chair and never pitch or toss,
Nor cuss, nor faint, nor die, while I'm extracting,
And never groan a bit about your loss;
If you can force your jaw to open wider,
Your tongue to keep away when I'm at work,
And hold them there while I drill that incisor,
And never spoil my technique with a jerk;

If you keep still while I move each bicuspid
To places where I think they'd better be
And tell you that you've been to stupid dentists
Whose work I'll rearrange for just my fee;
If you then pay the bill which I will send you
At once, nor murmur of an overcharge -
Yours is the world and everything that's in it,
Because you are the only one at large!

Princeton Star, 1 December 1922

Abandoned Mascot Mine

Chapter 17: The Dead Horse Transformed

This song is an example of how a local incident gets transformed by one or two of its participants into verse and song, as a sort of joke, and how it gets remembered and transformed to become the stuff of local folklore or legend.

It's also the story of a song, made locally in the earliest days of the settlement of the valley. We first came upon it in a song collected by Phil Thomas in Princeton in 1963, titled "There's Gold in the Tulameen".

> Oh there's gold in the Tulameen, there's platinum in the sand
> Berries for the pickin', why wander o'er the land?
> There's grouse upon the mountain and deer come to the door -
> You're welcome dear old-timer, don't wander any more.
>
> Paddy packed a bean sack, also a bale of hay,
> Murphy packed a bottle, but drank it on the way.
> Never trust a stranger, how plausible it seems –
> There's many a man from Jerusalem upon the Tulameen.

Art Shenton, a long-time resident of the area and a local versifier was the author of *Similkameen Tales* (1966). The first piece in his book, "Similkameen", has as its second and third stanzas:

> There is gold along these rivers
> And Platinum in the sand,
> Why travel any further
> This is a promised land.
>
> There is grouse upon the hillsides
> There is deer outside your door
> Build your cabin here Pardner
> You could not ask for more.

These lines were widely known in Princeton, perhaps through "Singing Jimmy" (a local character, known for his drinking and singing and himself memorialized in verses of the same name by Shenton).

It is a curious song, with only two verses – yet it had been remembered. We were intrigued, but didn't try to unravel the mystery until we began researching song material for the CD "Now It's Called Princeton". In the process, we came across, in the Princeton Archives, a small business card for the Riverside Motel, with the words of Shenton's first verse printed on the back. The card was undated, but looked to be from the 1930s.

But what of the second verse? The man who sang it for Thomas knew nothing about it. Who were "Paddy", and "Murphy", where were they going, and what was the relevance of the last couplet (which seemed at first glance to be offensive)? No one knew.

Our investigation of the local paper soon turned up a set of words that mentioned Murphy, one of the characters in Thomas's version of the verse. They were by W.H. Holmes, a well-known local man, who had settled in the Tulameen valley in the last days of the Granite Creek gold rush of 1885. His set ran as follows:

> There was an hydraulic upon the Tulameen,
> So rich in gold and platinum, the richest ever seen.
> It was managed by Thompson and he's so very keen
> He'd make you work your Dead Horse upon the Tulameen.
>
> Chorus
> It's no use in grumbling, you know it was a fake;
> You put your trust in Thompson, he's sure to burst you flat.
> He's sure to burst you flat, boys, no matter how you try,
> Or he'll send you to New Westminster to pine away and die.
>
> The leading men were Murphy and Donald Rankin;
> They could survey, grade or carpenter to any other thing.
> The rest of them were miners, the finest ever seen;
> But they were working out their Dead Horse upon the Tulameen.

There was Johnny Amberty and big Pete Gunderson,
Chinaman, the whip sawyer, and John L. Sullivan.
They all of them talk of what they might have been,
But they were working out their Dead Horse upon the Tulameen.

There's Murphy, an ex-sheriff, he came from Nevada;
When he gets you in the corner don't mind what he says,
For if you do, although he is no ways mean,
He'll play you for a sucker, boys, upon the Tulameen.

He walks about the claim to see the work is done
But when the dinner bell rings, you bet your life he'll come,
Except he's up the creek fishing in the stream,
But he's working out his Dead Horse upon the Tulameen.

There's Holmes an Englishman from famous Lancashire,
And in this blasted country he's working out for hire,
He's up on the hills felling ties so green,
But he's working out his Dead Horse upon the Tulameen.

The boarding house was first class the finest ever seen;
Sometimes eggs, but mostly pork and beans,
Except when the Indians, who came seldom I do fear,
They bring the boys a treat of a few legs of deer.

Now my song is ended, the harvest is past,
We've buried our blooming Dead Horse at last,
So everyone be careful by what you have seen,
Don't run another dead Horse upon the Tulameen.

This was the song as it appeared in the *Princeton Star* on Christmas Day, 1930 and it was to be sung, said the paper, to the tune of "Son of a Gambolier". It was the version we recorded on the CD. But it again raised more questions, and more names – Thompson, Murphy, Donald Rankin, Johnny Amberty, Pete Gunderson, "Chinaman, the whip sawyer", John L. Sullivan, and Holmes himself.

Some things were clear: these men were working on a gold and platinum claim on the Tulameen River using the hydraulic method (of high-pressure hoses blasting water at cliff faces to bring down material for sluicing). The "Dead Horse" comes from the phrase "working for a dead horse", meaning, "working to pay off debts", but might also refer to the name of the claim.

The claim was managed by Thompson, and the other names are of workers on the claim. We can identify "Judge Murphy". He was Thomas Murphy, and he had arrived in Granite Creek in 1886 following a very colourful life in the US, Australia and other places. He died in Tulameen at the age of 88 and is buried there in an unmarked grave. He had in fact been a sheriff in Nevada, but he appears never to have been a judge.

Diane Sterne, the historian of Coalmont, helps us with the rest:

> Big Pete is Pete Gunderson who was another Granite original. He was a miner and I believe from Norway. The Chinaman was probably Frenchy. No one knows what his real name was. It was common for white people to jump the claims of the Chinese, so he changed his name to Frenchy because 'no one ever jumped a Frenchman's claim'. Frenchy was good friends with all these fellows and his home was where the Rice ranch is today. Thompson was W.T. Thompson who owned a store, bar and ran the post office (all in one building) in Granite in 1888. He was from the States and his wife, Ida, was from Ontario. They had a daughter named Clover Gray. John L. Sullivan was a miner, a partner with Thomas Murphy in 1891. Donald Rankin was an early miner at Granite. Holmes was Walton Holmes (Walt Smart's grandfather) who was from Lancashire, England and had been well educated. "

The story of the Dead Horse now makes some kind of sense: the name "Murphy" is common to both songs and the first couplet of the "There's Gold in the Tulameen" suggests an expedition. The second couplet is still opaque.

Our next stroke of luck in retracing the tale of the Dead Horse came with a further visit to the Archives. We found yet another reference to the song, from the paper of 14 May 1920, and thus some ten years earlier than the Holmes song. It ran as follows:

The "Dead Horse" of the Tulameen
A Dirge, by Hemlock Joe

Come gather round the campfire, boys, and listen to my song,
While I tell you of the dead horse, boys, I will not keep you long.
'Tis of that crew, boys, who went up in the spring
To work out a dead horse upon the Tulameen.

Murphy packed up the bean sack, some twenty pounds or more,
Big Pete he packed the flour supply, of pounds that were three score;
For we were very hungry, boys, and looked so very lean,
As we went to work our dead horse, upon the Tulameen.

Pat he packed the bottle, boys, but he drank it on the way
And he left us very thirsty, boys, when we stopped at the close of day;
For it was very hard work, climbing against the stream,
To work out that dead horse upon the Tulameen.

We had men of many nations, men from near and far;
There were men from the famous Cariboo, and men from Cassiar;
They were indeed a motley crowd, the strangest I have seen
But they were working on a dead horse upon the Tulameen.

There were men from the railroad, so fond of getting drunk,
As they used to do in other days, when they worked for Onderdonk.
They ate up the grub, boys, with appetites so keen,
While working out their dead horse upon the Tulameen.

The weather was bad, boys; and we had neither house nor tent,
Until a pious Chinaman one to the company lent
For it was mighty hard, boys, the nights were cold and keen
While we were working out a dead horse upon the Tulameen.

> But now the summer is over, boys, its hardships they are past;
> And that confounded dead horse, we have worked it out last,
> And we are going down the river as poor as when in spring,
> We began to work our dead horse upon the Tulameen.
>
> My song is now ended; its moral you can see
> Never run a store bill nor go upon the spree,
> For all men are not honest, though plausible they seem
> Neither in Jerusalem nor on the Tulameen.

Here was our first couplet (stanza 2), and our last couplet (stanza 8)! The story is at last making sense. Diane Sterne adds the following:

> All of these men (including Thompson) were very good friends with each other. They had a tight-knit community. The Onderdonk reference: After the Onderdonk railway contract was finished, the leftover supplies at a closed commissary were sold at cheap prices and Holmes, Thompson, a man named Ferguson and a man named Newland all bought them and packed them in to Granite Creek. Jim Newland got shot shortly after arriving at Granite so his connection with the area was short lived. The other men and the men mentioned in the song became lasting friends. I believe they all made a decent living with their mining ventures and believe the song was written in jest. I doubt any of these men went hungry. "

The paper also published below the poem its own explanation, as follows:

> The "Dead Horse" of the Tulameen
>
> To the miners of Granite Creek the seasons of '90-91 were not of a character from a mining point of view to either fill the miner's purse or his stomach. In fact, things had come to such a pass that one, of two things had to be done. Men had either to emigrate or starve. The principal

storekeeper had not enough of flour in his store to bate [sic] a rat trap, and his credit with the wholesale people was practically nil. It is all very well for well fed people to talk about the beauties of Christianity and the soothing influence of religion, but hungry men are apt to look upon Christianity as a windy, unsatisfying quality, and religion as only soothing to those who received its benefits - let us say through the contribution box. But we will leave this subject to the clergy, and state that although the merchant was not a Christian, but a Levite of the inner temple, yet in those dark days he acted as uncle to the miner, receiving such articles of jewelry as he had and giving him beans, yes, straight beans, in return.

But hard times make people suspicious, and besides the man whose hearing was good might have heard something drop about his time, and to the credit of mankind be it said it always does drop at such times like rain, upon the famishing traveler in the desert. The good news that had dropped upon the camp was to the effect that certain charitably disposed gentlemen, living in and around New Westminster, had concluded to relieve the distress of the district by digging drain or ditch from the upper Tulameen to some point where gold and platinum would be fund [found], but failing to find precious metals it might serve as an irrigating ditch for the farmer when he should see fit to visit these parts or able to find any farming land. Men were at once engaged and sent up the river to begin work. Such was the beginning of this great enterprise, born in the midst of want, trouble and bad weather. A local poet, "Hemlock Joe," has celebrated the event in homely verse and of course the term "dead horse" means working out old bills. *Princeton Star*, 14 May 1920

We have solved one mystery, and found two more. Who was the "principal storekeeper" who was "not a Christian" but "a Levite of the inner temple", and what does this latter epithet mean? Levites were a priestly caste of Jews, and Levi, as well as being a common first and last name, was at the time a slang term for Jew. The inner temple reference might be to the locus of priestly service, or the whole phrase might be a reference to an English Jewish lawyer, whose chambers were at the Inner Temple, in London. Neither the 1891 nor the 1901 Census show any Jewish storekeeper in Granite Creek or in Princeton. The storekeeper appears from the 1920 report to have acted as a pawnbroker. What has this to do with lack of honesty, implied in the last verse (and in the last line of the opening song)?

A further newspaper clue arrived, from 1926. In that year, a young placer miner made a huge cleanup in platinum on the Tulameen: the *Princeton Star* headline screamed "Platinum Mining on Tulameen; Old "Dead Horse" Causes Sensation".

> Following the account of the find and a visit with his friends to the claim, the newspaper editor goes on to identify the location and its history:
>
> The wonderful strike by Mr. Sootheran is on the property known to all oldtimers as the "Dead Horse" placer claim, but is now known officially as Placer Lease Number so and so. The recent excitement brings back memories of days gone by to several oldtimers who are still with us, particularly to Mr. Walton H. Holmes, Judge Murphy and Johnny Amberty, who all worked on the "Dead Horse" at various times. In fact Mr. Holmes was one of a party who prospected and finally staked the property for Mr. W. J. Thompson, who was a brother-in-law of Mr. A. E. Howse.
>
> Mr. Thompson ran a store in Granite Creek, but engaged in a little mining promotion as well. In 1892 the "Dead Horse" was staked and a Company composed mostly of New Westminster men commenced to operate it. A sawmill was put in to saw lumber for flumes, cabins, sluice boxes, etc.

But the venture did not turn out to be a success. Little did the then operators think that the despised "white gold" would one day be worth five and ten times the value of the yellow gold and that their claim would one day be the means of focusing the eyes of the world upon the Tulameen as containing what are probably the world's most important reserves of platinum.

Mr. Holmes composed quite a lengthy poem on the "Dead Horse". Nearly every man who worked out a dead horse (old store bill) was honored by a verse in it. A much cut down and toned-down version of the poem appeared in the May 14th, 1920, issue of the *Princeton Star.* The poem was credited "Hemlock Joe" the nom de plume of the genial and popular Judge Murphy. It appears that the judge composed the final verse, and in that way was given credit for the whole poem.
Princeton Star, 10 June 1926

So it now appears that the events occurred in 1892. W.H. Holmes made a song about it, with a verse for each of the participants. It was then cut-down and toned-down (by who, and why?) for a version that appeared in the paper in 1920. Another song (the 1930 version, the first one printed here, with an almost entirely different set of verses, except for the final line of each verse) was claimed by Holmes, set to a named tune and published ten years later. Finally, it was one stanza of the "Hemlock" set that was remembered (or should we say dis-remembered?) in 1963.

But wait once more. Once more the Archives were searched, and lo and behold, yet another mention of the song appeared, this time in 1900! A Christmas Concert was held in that year, and in the 29 December issue of the paper was a report of a "Christmas entertainment". Various party pieces were performed that night, including a recitation by Albert Irwin, called "Dead Horse on the Tulameen".

> The noticeable feature of the evening's entertainment were [sic] the different selections which were adapted to this particular locality. "Working Out the Dead Horse on the Tulameen", by Bert Irwin, was a local skit which recalled bygone days to many old timers in the audience and is a piece that is always appreciated."

According to the 1911 Census, Albert Irwin was a 22-year-old Princeton resident, and would be 23 the following month. However, his name does not appear in the 1901 Census, either in Princeton or in Granite Creek. How did he come to know of events that occurred eight years earlier when he was 13 years old? There is no record of his family – in the 1911 Census he is described as "head" of his household, and he was married, but there is no census record for his wife.

From this brief note, it appears that the piece was well-known and was "always appreciated", and Irwin recited it with "Judge" Thomas Murphy, then 58 years old, in the audience.

Well, there you have it: two songs and a poem, all somehow connected with one expedition up one river to work at a claim. Though the unraveling takes time, it gives us an incomparable view of the lived experiences of the people involved – a sense of the very small community, sharing, at its Christmas get-together, an even smaller joke. I doubt we would call events of nine year ago "bygone days", but those nine years in the Tulameen and Princeton areas were the difference between living in a tent and living in a real town with a newspaper.

The story of the "Dead Horse" is not over – several long-time Princeton residents still carry the short "There's Gold in the Tulameen" version in their heads. Dawn Johnson, daughter of Art Shenton, remembers hearing her parents singing it. When we asked Lori Thomas how she knew it she replied, "It seems like I've always known it." She and her mother are descendants of John Fall Allison, one of the original settlers in the valley. They remember hearing it from Singing Jimmy, a local character reputed to have been a vaudeville ventriloquist. Knowing the song is somehow a marker for being descended from Princeton pioneers.

Manning Park 1943. The Allan Gill Collection

CHAPTER NOTES

Abbreviations Used

Blake	Don Blake, *Blakeburn: From Dust to Dust.* Penticton, 1985: Skookum Publications Ltd.
Currie	Laurie Currie, *Princeton 120 Years.* Princeton, 1990
Goodfellow	John Goodfellow, *The Story of the Similkameen* Princeton, 1958: Princeton Centennial Committee
Grainger	M. Allerdale Grainger, *Riding the Skyline Trail.* Victoria, 1994: Horsdal & Schubart Publishers Ltd.
Malanchuk	Terry Malanchuk, *Blakeburn: British Columbia's Forgotten Ghost Town.* 2nd rev. ed., Chilliwack, 2008: Malanchuk Publications
PJTColl	PJ Thomas Collection, Aural History Archives of BC, Victoria
Princeton CD	Jon Bartlett & Rika Ruebsaat, "Now It's Called Princeton: Songs and Poems of BC's Upper Similkameen". Princeton Traditional Music Society, 2008
PS	*Princeton Star*
SPNW	PJ Thomas, *Songs of the Pacific Northwest.* Surrey, 2nd ed., 2006 (1st ed., 1979): Hancock House
SS	*Similkameen Star*
Sterne	Diane Sterne, *White Gold and Black Diamonds: The History of Granite Creek and Coalmont.* Coalmont, 2011

Preface

Thomas Collection: (hereafter PJTColl) Phil Thomas' collection of 499 items from 102 informants, made between the years of 1954 and 1975, and now lodged in the Aural History Archives of BC, Victoria.

Chapter 1: Popular Song and Verse Traditions of the Early 20th Century

Other Men's Flowers. London, 1944: Jonathan Cape; **the first radio ad**: PS, 16 Oct 1924; **Burns Nights**: see Jon Bartlett & Rika Ruebsaat, "Robert Burns In Princeton: An Exploration" at http://jonandrika.org/; **Population of Princeton**, 1918: PS, 18 Oct 1918

Chapter 2: The Settlement of The Similkameen

A Song of BC: Another version of this poem was found in the Dave Taylor fonds in the Princeton Archives; **"Haw Haw, By Jove variety of Englishman"**: SS 29 Mar 1912 referred to in a letter to the editor entitled "English Ranchers Tumbling into Tulameen"; **The Greater Briton in England:** Arthur Stringer (1874-1950), a published poet, born in Ontario, who moved to New Jersey in 1921; **Estelle Kerr quotes**: "Beside the Tulameen", SS 27 Aug 1915; **Walton Hugh Holmes coming into Granite Creek**: Goodfellow, p. 51. Also found in

Diane Sterne's *White Gold and Black Diamonds;* **Father Pat**: Jerome Mercier, *Father Pat: A Hero of the Far West.* Gloucester, 1909: Minchin & Gibbs 1909; **Welldo**: Sterne, p. 49, "The Little Town that Wasn't"; **Princeton Businesses, 1901**: 4 general mercantile stores, 3 hotels, 2 butcher shops, 1 tin & gunsmith, 4 livery & feed stables, 1 news stand, 1 barber shop, 3 laundries, 1 lawyer, 1 doctor, 1 mining engineer, 1 provincial land surveyor, 1 real estate office, 1 printing & newspaper office, 1 bakery, 1 blacksmith shop, 4 contractors & builders, 4 lumber dealers, 1 coal dealer, 1 wood yard, 1 assay office, 1 gov't office, "unrepresented" – bank, hardware, druggist, brewery, jeweller & watchmaker, tailor, cigar & tobacconist, shoemaker, harness & saddlery, restaurant: SS 26 Oct 1901. **Princeton Businesses, 1909**: 4 general stores, 3 hotels, 3 bakers, 1 restaurant, 2 fruit & candy stores, 1 drug & stationery store, 2 livery stables, 1 blacksmith shop, 1 bank, 1 butcher shop, 1 watchmaker, 1 tailoring & renovating works, 1 plumbing & tinshop, 1 skating rink, 1 billiard hall, 2 barber shops, 3 laundries, 2 brickyards, 1 harness & shoemaker, 1 confectioner, 1 photographer (non-resident), 1 surveyor (non-resident), 1 doctor, 1 newspaper & 2nd hand store, coming (opening for lawyer & architect) SS 15 Dec 1909; **Al Johnston quote**: "Kloochman's Race Feature of Pioneer Celebrations: Al Johnston Reminisces on the Good Old Days", SS, 11 Aug 1938; **Chinook jargon**: see George Gibbs, *Dictionary of the Chinook Jargon.* New York, 1863: Cramoisy Press. There are also many online dictionaries; **To the Princeton Bachelor Maids**: below the copy we inspected are written the words "a load of old hasbeens"; **"leaving 381 acres of the most worthless land..."**: Cole Harris, *Making Native Space: Colonialism, Resistance, and Reserves in British Columbia.* Vancouver, 2002 UBC Press, p. 213; **"should not be tucked away on reserves...",** Harris, *Making Native Space,* p.87; **Time by the forelock**: "Coalmont, the Town of Opportunity", *Coalmont Courier* 17 Jun 1912; **Blakeburn tramway**: see Malanchuk and Blake; **The body of William Stevenson**: SS 10 Sep 1915

Chapter 3: Boosterism

Wetherell quotation: Donald G. Wetherell & Irene RA Kmet, *Town Life: Main Street and the Evolution of Small Town Alberta, 1880-1947.* Edmonton, 1995: The University of Alberta Press; **It Isn't your Town – It's You:** This poem appeared three times in Princeton papers, sometimes with the title, "Your Town As You Like It", 18 Dec 1914, 13 Apr 1923, 22 Sep 1927. Also found in *North Tonawanda Evening News,* 20 Jan 1920, *Ocean City News,* 6 Oct 1923; **"Solid citizens came to Princeton...", :** Currie, p. 79; **Out Where the West Begins**: Arthur Chapman (1873-1935), reporter and author of two books of poetry; *Out Where The West Begins* (1917) and *Cactus Center* (1921). The poem was so popular that the Australians adopted it, changing it to "That's where the Outback begins."; **How Some Easterners Regard Us**: James Barton Adams (1843-1918) , one of the few cowboy poets published prior to the 1900s, with the book, *Breezy Western Verse* (1889). He was included in several collections, including John A. Lomax's *Songs of the Cattle Train and Cow Camp* (1919)

Chapter 4: The Weekly Press

"Editor a Union man": SS, 1 Apr 1908; **Background information on Lowery**, see Bronson A. Little's "Robert T Lowery: Editor, Publisher and Printer" in *British Columbia Historical News*, Spring 1998; **Background information on Taylor**, see Nick Mills' article in *Similkameen News Leader*, 5 May 2009, p. 9; **John Goodfellow**, the first historian of the Similkameen (see Goodfellow above), took over the editorial chair from Dave Taylor on his leaving the country for China in 1938, and yielded it up in 1946 on Taylor's return; **the first issue** of the *Coalmont Courier* was 6 May 1912; **"One by one…":** SS, 4 Feb 1937; **He does not advertise:** also in *The Altamont Enterprise*, 2 Jun 1999, *The Orangeville Banner*, 11 May 1911; *The Spectator*, 1911; *Northern Territory Times & Gazette*, 18 Oct 1919 and *Pine Plains Register & Herald*, 1 Mar 1928; **A Wise Geezer**, also in *Cass City Chronicle*, 5 May 1916; an Andover paper, 1 July 1921; and the *Winthrop News*, 7 May 1925; the tune is possibly "The Red Haired Boy" or "Turkey in the Straw"; **Send It In** also in *The Beaver*, Jan 1921, *Grapurchat*, Radford State Normal School for Women (Virginia), Feb. 1921, *The Wisconsin Alumni Magazine*, Jan 1923, *The Racquet*, la Crosse, Wisconsin, 24 Oct 1923, and *The Missionary Worker*, 23 Feb 1934; **Kindly Mail Check**, also in 16 other papers from the *Ellensburg Dawn*, 7 Dec 1900 to the *Flesherton Advance* of 15 Jan 1936; **That Towel**, also in *Sausalito News*, 13 December 1889, *Tuapika Times*, 30 Apr 1890, *Otago Times*, 19 Mar 1891, *Geneva Advertiser*, 3 May 1893, *Daily Public Ledger* (Maysville, KY), 23 May 1899 derived from the *New York Sun*; *Hartford (*KY) *Republican*, 4 Oct 1901; *Northern Territory Times* (Darwin, NT) 17 Jun 1932; the cartoon is from Maggie Holtzberg-Call,. *The Lost World of the Craft Printer*. Urbana & Chicago, 1992: University of Illinois Press; **The Newspaper Guy**: another verse: I see a man strut through a jam in the hall/Take a seat 'mid the speakers and chat with them all/"Is this Hoover?" I ask, "that the crowd he defies?"/"No," someone says, "He's one of the newspaper guys."

Chapter 5: Sports

Sing a Song of Baseball: PS 27 June 1919; **Spiel**: short for "bonspiel", a curling tournament. The word is from the gaelic; **Declaration of Independence**: perhaps from Eston, Saskatchewan; **Lacrosse**: Currie, p. 66

Chapter 6: Mining

More information concerning Blakeburn: consult Blake and Malanchuk; **Jimmy Colly**: the song is followed by "published by the National Song Bureau and copyrighted by James L. Colly". The tune is "Springtime in the Rockies", Robert Sauer, 1926. **Inflammatory columns**: The first such column was published 23 November 1932, and the editor at that time was Dave Taylor. **Population figures**: These are drawn from the Decennial censuses of 1901 and 1911

Chapter 7: To the Coast

The Prayer of the Similkameen Prospector: the poem is a parody of the Litany from the *Anglican Book of Common Prayer* that contains such lines as "From lightning and tempest, from earthquake, fire and flood; from plague, pestilence and famine; from battle and murder, and from sudden death, Good Lord deliver us. **Wait Till the Railroad's Finished**: to the tune of "Wait Till the Sun Shines, Nellie", music by Harry Von Tilzer, lyrics by Andrew B. Sterling, and published 1905, to become a pop song of the day; **Mr. Gallagher and Mr. Shean**: Vaudeville was a revue-style of theatrical entertainment popular in the United States and Canada from the early 1880s until the early 1930s. It originated in New York City and by the latter years of the 19th century had spread throughout North America. This version of "Mister Gallagher and Mister Shean" is a parody of the original song of the same name, which was one of the most famous songs to come out of vaudeville. The original was first performed by the duo of Ed Gallagher and Al Shean in the early 1920s and contained jokes typical of the time as well as the lampooning of current fads and events. The song was so famous that it gave rise to numerous parodies and the refrain at the end of each verse, "Positively, Mr. Gallagher, absolutely, Mr. Shean" became a well-known catchphrase for many years thereafter. **Relief camp**: during World War II the abandoned relief camp, renamed Tashme, was used as an internment camp for the Japanese: it is now called "Sunshine Valley", and no trace of the relief camp/Tashme remains; **Three Brothers hike, July 1931**: Edna Dignan Slater, "Three Men on a Mountain: Dave Taylor Remembers", *British Columbia Historical News*, Spring 1997.

Chapter 8: The Coming of the Car
"for one hundred years…", Currie, p. 38; **Thomas anecdote**: from the cutline to a photo in the Dave Taylor fonds, Princeton Archives; **"Autogarage"** ad, SS, 15 Aug 1913; **Grainger**, p. 31; **Henry Ford**, from *The Listening Post*; **"The money that used to circulate…"**, Grainger, p. 25; **The Joy Rider**: by F. J. Oulette; **Ask the Man Who Owns One:** C. Wiles Hallock, a.k.a. Hale Wentworth; **Teaching Them to Drive**: also in *Deschutes Pine Echoes*, Dec 1931 and *Daily Herald*, Chicago, 31 Jun 1931; **The Village Motorsmith**: also in *New Castle News*, New Castle, PA, 26 July 1928 and also remembered by someone in North Dakota.

Chapter 9: The Valley and the War
"The Union Jack": first published in 1901 in Barlow Cumberland's *History of* the Union Jack, where it was credited to an anonymous writer signing himself "St. George". It appeared in the *Victoria Colonist* 16 Dec 1910 and was a recommended poem for use in the teaching of History in Ontario high schools, appearing in the *Ontario Teachers Manuals: History, 1915*; **"Hoch der Kaiser"**, *Hedley Gazette*, 28 Jul 1910, again on 20 Aug 1914 and 11 Nov 1915. The Teddy Roosevelt version appeared in SS, 13 Oct 1916. **'coal box':** a slang name for a heavy shell, from the large quantity of black smoke from the explosion. Another name for such a shell was a "Jack Johnson" (the first black American world heavyweight boxing champion)

Chapter 10: Prohibition
"The Rumseller", PJTColl #473, 3 Sept 1964, from Fred Thompson at Heffley

Creek; **"Alone on the depot platform…"**, also PS, 27 Jan 1922 and *Dayton Review*, 6 May 1937; **1920 referendum results**: votes for control/ votes for continued prohibition, drawn from the *Star*.: Princeton 191/87, Allenby 50/10, Copper Mountain 87/13, Coalmont 16/15, Hedley 67/27, Tulameen 11/12; **"Come All You Coal Miners"**, PJTColl #123, 1 Oct 1963, from Bob Baird of Princeton from SPNW, p. 95; **"Why Man Lives A Long Life":** also found in Alan Dundes, *Never Try to Teach a Pig to Sing*, noting three sets from 1947 to 1974. Alpheus Mason suggests in *Pillar of the Law* that the author was the book's subject, Harlan Fiske Stone, a Justice of the US Supreme Court.

Chapter 11: Making Ends Meet

"Heavens Enough for Him", with the character a doctor, in I. Arthur King (ed.), *The Doctor's Domicile*, Akron, OH & Chicago, Il, 1905; *South African Medical Record*, 1905 ("We are indebted for the following to Dr. Clayton, of Heilbron, who picked it up in the house of a Canadian settler whom he was visiting professionally. It is on a card bearing the imprint of a Canadian drug firm)"; with the character (as here) a grocer, also in *Cato Citizen*, Cato. NY., 14 Jan 1916; *Daily Palladium*, 14 Oct 1922; as a blacksmith, on a South Dakota business card, 1940; *New Castle News*, New Castle, PA, 2 Feb 1916; U. of Iowa, 1916; **"Where there are tubs of rich milk":** Grainger, p. 78; **"There's Gold in the Tulameen"**, PJTColl #122, 1 Oct 1963 from Bob Baird, Princeton.

Chapter 12: The Second World War

"Make It Do": also in the *Cariboo Observer*, 27 March 1943; **"Somebody's Son"**, in G.L. Creed's *For Freedom*. Toronto, Vancouver, 1942: J.M. Dent & Sons (Canada) Ltd.; **Tommy Douglas quote**: Tommy Douglas, *The Making of a Socialist*. Edmonton, 1982: University of Alberta Press, p. 125

Chapter 13: A Pot Pourri of Topical Verses

Lone Grouse Supper characters: thanks to Diane Sterne, the historian of Coalmont: personal email, 6 Feb 2011; **We love the place, O God**: hymn in the Anglican hymnbook composed by Isaac Van Vleck Flagler (1844-1909); **Dominion Day**: this poem is an acrostic where the first letter of each line spells our "The Great Dominion" vertically; **Shem, Ham and Japhet:** the sons of Noah in the Old Testament. **Trouble on the Similkameen**: the results of the election: Shatford 298, Curtis 200, Winkler 29: see *Electoral History of British Columbia 1871-1986*.Victoria: Elections British Columbia, 1988.

Chapter 14: Earning a Living

Strike Committee's demands: compare the demands with the recommended BC Loggers' Association pay rates, as published in SS, 26 Feb 1908: – per mo. Chef (large camp) $65; white cooks $60; flunky $30; man & wife as cook & flunky $80; Chinese cook 1st $45; Chinese cook 2nd $35; string teamster (2 horses) $40; single boy $20; Daily men $5.35/wk; blacksmith $3/d; bl helper $2/d; boomman 1st $3/d; 2nd $2.50/d; greaser $2.25/d; faller 1st $3.50/d; 2nd $3; undercutter

$3.50; bucker $3; woodcutter (roader) $2.50; wood splitter $2; head skidder $3.25; skidroad man $2; swamper $2.50; donkey engineer $3.25; donkey fireman $2.50; hook tender $4; rigging slinger $3; chaser for yarder $3; chokerman $3; signalman $2.25; sniper $2.50; knotter $2.50; line horse man $2.50; dog up man $2.50; PF man $3.25; **The Workers' Song**: the cartoon is from Joyce L. Kornbluh (ed., intro.). *Rebel Voices: An I.W.W. Anthology.* Ann Arbor, 1972: University of Michigan Press; **She Has No Occupation**: The *Minneapolis Morning Tribune*, of 23 February 1910 ran an article outlining for the would-be enumerators for the upcoming census how to treat women's work, thusly: "In the case of a woman doing housework in her own home, without salary or wages, and having no other employment, the entry is to be that she has no occupation." Elsie Duncan Yale, *Sunshine* magazine; "One day the census taker called and wrote down in a book./ and so, as I was hanging 'round I thought I'd take a look./He had our names and ages all, and put down Dad's vocation,/ and after mother's name he wrote she had "No Occupation.". There follows five more stanzas very similar to the set printed here. Yale must have taken two stabs at the theme.

Chapter 15: The Natural World

"Environed by stern mountains..." from "Evening on the Similkameen" by Susan Allison (aka Stratton Moir) SS, 7 Apr 1915

Chapter 16: Just for Fun

"Served Him Right", also in *Whitehaven Gazette*, 27 May 1897 and dozens more papers, some varying the culture (i.e. Indian versions, with "He didn't like my curries...", and note a Yiddish version:He didn't like my salt beef/ And he didn't like my cake/My *kichel* were too hard.../Not like his mother used to make. //I didn't make the *borsht* right/He left the *cholent* stew./I didn't wash his *gatkes*... /The way his mother used to do.//I pondered for an answer/I was looking for a clue./Then I turned around and gave him a *potch*... /Like his mother used to do. (*potch:: smack; kichel: small round plain biscuit; cholent: potted meat and vegetables simmered overnight; borsht: beetroot soup; gatkes: underpants)*

Chapter 17: The Dead Horse Transformed

"There's Gold in the Tulameen", PJTColl #122, 1 Oct 1963 from Bob Baird, Princeton; **Shenton's book**: Art Shenton, *Similkameen Tales*, Princeton, 1966; **Princeton CD**: the tune given is the same tune as "I'm a Ramblin' Wreck from Georgia Tech" or "The Man That Waters the Worker's Beer", derived ultimately from a printed source of about 1870; **Diane Sterne, the historian of Coalmont**: personal email, 6 Feb 2011; **Hemlock Joe version**: PS, 14 May 1920; **"After the Onderdonk railway contract was finished...":** Andrew Onderdonk (1848-1905), was hired by the CPR to manage the building of the railway through the BC mountains. As such he was responsible for hiring and feeding the workers.

Sources

Primary Sources

Dave Taylor fonds in the Princeton Archives
Coalmont Courier
Hedley Gazette
Princeton Star
Similkameen Star
Census, 1891
Census, 1901
Census, 1911

Secondary Sources

Bartlett, Jon & Rika Ruebsaat, "Robert Burns In Princeton: An Exploration" at http://jonandrika.org/

Blake, Don. *Blakeburn: From Dust to Dust.* Penticton, 1985: Skookum Publications Ltd.

Creed, G.L. *For Freedom.* Toronto, Vancouver, 1942: J.M. Dent & Sons (Canada) Ltd.

Cumberland, Barlow. *History of the Union Jack*, Toronto, 1900: William Briggs

Currie, Laurie. *Princeton 120 Years.* Princeton, 1990

Douglas, Tommy. *The Making of a Socialist.* Edmonton, 1982: University of Alberta Press

Dundes, Alan & Carl R. Pagter. *Never Try to Teach a Pig to Sing: Still More Urban Folklore from the Paperwork Empire.* Detroit, 1991: Wayne State University Press

Electoral History of British Columbia 1871-1986. Victoria, 1988: Elections British Columbia

Gibbs, George. *Dictionary of the Chinook Jargon.* New York, 1863: Cramoisy Press

Goodfellow, John. *The Story of the Similkameen.* Princeton, 1958: Princeton Centennial Committee

Grainger, M. Allerdale. *Riding the Skyline Trail.* Victoria, 1994: Horsdal & Schubart Publishers Ltd.

Harris, Cole. *Making Native Space: Colonialism, Resistance, and Reserves in British Columbia.* Vancouver, 2002: UBC Press

Holtzberg-Call, Maggie. *The Lost World of the Craft Printer.* Urbana & Chicago, 1992: University of Illinois Press

Kornbluh, Joyce L. (ed., intro.). *Rebel Voices: An I.W.W. Anthology.* Ann Arbor, 1972: University of Michigan Press

Little, Bronson A. "Robert T. Lowery: Editor, Publisher and Printer" in *British Columbia Historical News*, Spring 1998

Malanchuk, Terry. *Blakeburn: British Columbia's Forgotten Ghost Town.* 2nd rev. ed., Chilliwack, 2008: Malanchuk Publications

Mills, Nick, "Dave Taylor" in *Similkameen News Leader*, 5 May 2009

Mercier, Jerome. *Father Pat: A Hero of the Far West.* Gloucester, 1909: Minchin & Gibbs 1909

Princeton History Book Committee. *Princeton: Our Valley.* Princeton, 2000

Slater, Edna Dignan. "Three Men on a Mountain: Dave Taylor Remembers", *British Columbia Historical News*, Spring 1997

Sterne, Diane. *White Gold and Black Diamonds: The History of Granite Creek and Coalmont.* Coalmont, 2011

Thomas, Philip J. *Songs of the Pacific Northwest.* Surrey, 2nd ed., 2006 (1st ed., 1979): Hancock House.

Wavell, A.P. *Other Men's Flowers.* London, 1944: Jonathan Cape

Wetherell, Donald G. & Irene RA Kmet, *Town Life: Main Street and the Evolution of Small Town Alberta, 1880-1947.* Edmonton, 1995: The University of Alberta Press

Recordings

Jon Bartlett & Rika Ruebsaat, "Now It's Called Princeton: Songs and Poems of BC's Upper Similkameen" (Princeton Traditional Music Society, 2008), available from the Society at princetonfestival@telus.net.

Bob Baird, "There's Gold in the Tulameen", PJTColl #122,

Bob Baird, "Come All You Coal Miners", PJTColl #123

Fred Thompson, "The Rumseller", PJTColl #473

Song, Poem, Movie Index

Mentioned

* *

Collection

(bold refers to song text)

Burns Supper in Hedley 1940s

Index of Names

General Index

Manning Park, 1943. The Allan Gill collection

Jon Bartlett & Rika Ruebsaat

Authors Jon Bartlett and Rika Ruebsaat are singers of traditional song, with a special interest in BC's social history. They have been singing and working together since 1975 and have been involved in every aspect of traditional music – singing, collecting, publishing, educating, producing radio programs, and organizing folk music societies and local traditional music festivals. They have produced a CD of traditional shanties and forebitters and three CD's of Canadian songs: Come to Me in Canada, The Green Fields of Canada, and The Young Man from Canada, a collection of British Columbia songs from the Phil Thomas Collection. They are the authors of many papers having to do with traditional song. Their website is at http://www3.telus.net/jonbartlett-rikaruebsaat/.

Their particular area of expertise is the song tradition of British Columbia. They have worked for many years with the late Phil Thomas, BC's pre-eminent folk song collector, and Bartlett is editor of the new edition of Thomas's Songs of the Pacific Northwest. Their recent move to Princeton, BC prompted them to begin research in the local archives for songs. This book grew out of their investigation of the newspapers preserved in the Princeton & District Museum and Archives, between the years 1900 and 1950. The first result of this research was their CD, Now It's Called Princeton: Songs and Poems from the Upper Similkameen, which contains 27 Similkameen songs and poems. They are active in the local Arts Council, Museum and History Society, and are planning further books drawing on the newspaper resources of the West Kootenays.

"Now It's Called Princeton: Songs and Poems of BC's Upper Similkameen"

The CD draws some of its material from the newspapers deposited in the Princeton Archives. These poems and songs also appear in this book, and they are as follows:

- The Hangup Stick
- Dead Horse Upon The Tulameen
- That Reminds Me
- A Song Of BC
- A Plea For Single Men
- A Midwinter Night's Dream
- That Towel
- The Blakeburn Song
- A Miner's Candlestick
- Wanted, a Railroad
- Wait Till the Railroad's Finished
- In My Dreams
- There's Gold in the Tulameen
- Princeton Friendship

Much of the rest of material was derived from Phil Thomas' collection project, and relates to Similkameen concerns and interests. The CD comes with a 24-pp. book with background on the songs and verses, archival photographs and information about song practices, the Princeton Traditional Music Society (which brought the CD into existence, and which runs an annual free festival of traditional music), and Phil Thomas and his collection and published books. The CD is available from the Society at princetonfestival@telus.net